Keira,
Many blessings,
Carol

MW00681188

Where All Our Journeys End:

Searching for the Beloved in Everyday Life

C. Lynn Anderson, D.Min., ACSW

© 2008 C. Lynn Anderson
All Rights Reserved.

No part of this publication may be reproduced, stored in a retrieval system, or transmitted, in any form or by any means, electronic, mechanical, photocopying, recording, or otherwise, without the written permission of the author.

First published by Dog Ear Publishing
4010 W. 86th Street, Ste H
Indianapolis, IN 46268
www.dogearpublishing.net

ISBN: 978-159858-554-4

This book is printed on acid-free paper.

Printed in the United States of America

Contents

Dedication

To
P.W.

I have missed you all my life.

Acknowledgements

I wish to thank all who have helped make this a special journey. This includes editing advice from Charles Burack, Ph.D, and the computer expertise of Toni Poole, who turned this computer illiterate into a semi-literate being. My gratitude to friends and family who supported and encouraged this process, especially Lenore Andres, Brenda Bartz, Jane Hayes, Mary McCoy, Cilla Payne, and Mary Raymer, who read various editions of this book and offered their feedback. Also, thank you to the people at The University of Creation Spirituality (Wisdom University) who continue to teach peace, healing, compassion, and justice-making. And finally, my blessings to all those individuals who have shared their stories with me in courage and trust and who continue to embody the spirit of healing.

FOREWORD

When I consciously began my spiritual journey in my early thirties, I had absolutely no idea what this process would mean to me and no idea as to the levels of transformation it would entail. Prior to this journey, I considered myself a lapsed agnostic — someone who had few spiritual convictions, but not committed to this lack of conviction. Yet perhaps under the surface was a belief in the Divine; there was definitely a connection to nature and the metaphysical, but my upbringing in the Methodist and Presbyterian churches did not address that as something spiritual. When my life was turned upside down by some difficult life circumstances, when I discovered I really wasn't in control of my life, and when my expectations continued to be shattered, I recognized it was time to explore a spiritual program. This was, by no means, a healthy "letting go" process, but more of an "I give up" experience.

I began doing all those things that a spiritual person was "supposed" to do: I prayed, meditated, read spiritual materials, began attending church, and allowed myself to open to the experiences of the Beloved. Once I committed to this openness and practiced my faith, I began to have mystical experiences which even further confirmed my belief. But after a few years, I became rather complacent regarding my commitment to the Divine — while I still practiced my beliefs, I did not allow my heart to be fully open to the experience of the Source. There was little enrichment in my spiritual program; there was little enrichment to my life in general.

But around the time I turned forty, my life was again thrown into chaos and I recognized I needed to examine my beliefs, my practices, and my faith. During this time, my relationship of seven years ended, which propelled me into a deep level of sorrow not only from that loss but also from previous losses that hadn't been fully grieved. I also experienced a level of human evil in another person that shook my very core. Moreover, at this time, I developed a spiritual relationship with a friend that was a merging of souls into the sacredness of the Divine. The transformation that took place during this time has been (and continues to be) a process of healing which has resulted in a rebirth of my spirit.

I had been introduced to Creation Spirituality and Matthew Fox's work during my early thirties through Unity Church. This spiritual program was incredible to me. In it I finally found a belief system and a community to which I could relate. With this discovery, I was also able to place into context the beauty, awe and mysticism, as well as the pain and sorrow, which I experienced as a child. There was finally a vocabulary, the *word* of the Beloved that touched me to my soul.

I have found this path to be one of incredible healing and transformation. For many years, my mantra has been, "Help me to give back to others as others have given to me," and in my roles of therapist and educator, I hope I have been able to do this. I have experienced so many blessings in my life — blessings of people, blessings of experiences, blessings of Spirit. Both my inner and outer works are about allowing the divinity within myself to help with the healing process of all others, including the Earth, the cosmos, and the universal soul. While spiritual growth is of the individual, it must also be about healing collectively. On personal, professional and community levels, I have become an activist for change –- the mystical and the prophetic. This work has resulted in these writings.

Our past and present mystics have provided us with a sense of immediacy, a sense of direction, and a sense of love, compassion, and healing. This book has been created for the purpose of doing my part in helping to transform in immanence and transcendence, for the purpose in life is to reach the stars and in reaching the stars, to touch one another in our divinity and our humanity. This is blessing and being blessed.

INTRODUCTION

We are in a crisis of epic proportions for we are so technologically advanced and yet so spiritually bereft. Terrorism is a mainstay throughout the world, and our wars are supposedly holy ones. The Earth is being destroyed through individual and systemic means — bombings, environmental holocaust, greed, territorialism, and consumerism. Our human rights are determined by those persons and groups in power who benefit from the very trampling of human lives and the human spirit. Our civil rights are being decimated by an administration fueled by greed, power, control, and self-righteousness.

Through our scientific advances, we can destroy the world many times over; we can alter genetics, soar into the atmosphere, and unite the world through telecommunications. How smug we are about such progress; how pleased we are in our so-called advancements. For if individuals wish to compete with their neighbors in a gluttony of ownership, surely nations are even more grandiose in their need to control, hoard, and justify more goods, more services, more guns, more oil, more land, more, more, more . . . .

Yet in our search for the ultimate experience — the biggest SUV, the most powerful gun, the grandest home, the greatest high — we ignore our origins and our most basic inner need, that of spirituality. For while we are technologically advanced into the age of adulthood, we are mere kindergartners in our spiritual development. For only one who is spiritually limited can justify war as holy; only one who is spiritually impotent can rape the environment as well as one another; only one who is so defeated spiritually can close his eyes to what is happening in the world today.

So how do we heal from the trauma and destruction that we have created? We must first accept responsibility for our part in what we have created and what we have harmed. For unless we accept responsibility, we will continue to blame others, ignore our own culpability, and continue in the path of annihilation. And in our responsibility, we need to return to our roots, for herein lies the solution. We can return to the depths of our very being by reconnecting and remembering ourselves as divine beings who have been given the blessing of co-creation. We have been birthed to create with the Ultimate Creator, to fulfill our destiny of goodness, compassion, and love; to heal ourselves, each other, the planet, and the cosmos. Past and present mystics are warning us that the time is now, for if we do not act to change the horrific path we have set forth for ourselves, we will be destroyed in a gigantic ending to the story of humanity, and perhaps, to the planet itself.

If we explore this course of action we've set forth for ourselves, we see that we have forgotten our ground in the light and the love of the Beloved; to that underlying dynamic connection to the mystical; to the joy, awe, passion, and love that underlies all of creation. How have we forgotten her? We have done so in our forgotten blessings, in our grandiosity and in our narcissism. If we do not change our ways, we will remain spiritually adrift in a sea of endless greed. Not in the solitude and the silence or the emptiness, not in the letting go and letting be, but in the destruction and void of connection. This is the shadow side, the darkness that remains hidden and which ferments in terror, pain, and abandonment. For without the roots of the blessings of awe and joy, we are sinking into the depths of destruction and evil. In this path, we are refusing to understand and connect with our own pain, the pain and sorrow of others, as well as the sorrow of the universe and of the Beloved. We allow so much suffering to exist, but we are doing so little to alleviate such pain. For where is our compassion? We need to be willing to delve into the darkness in order to heal; we must delve into the darkness to expand our human selves into the creativity of our divine selves.

So what will it take to awaken us? It will take an opening of our hearts, a connection to life and to living, a remembrance of the underlying passion and compassion of the universe which is genetically encoded in each and every one of us. For we are all made up of the particles from the very beginning of time, those atoms of creation manifested by Goddess for she is within and without all of existence. This is our depth, our origin, our root. This is the mysticism of the interconnection of all sentient and non-sentient beings.

This book explores this very need — our connection to the Divine and to all that has been graced by her. She is always there, awaiting us to return to her in our God-given destiny of compassion and love. In these writings, we will seek to remember who and what we are in our blessings of being a human entrusted to co-create; a human being that is a divine spark of the divine essence; a human being that loves, passionately loves, all of creation. For the Divine is our ultimate destiny, where all our journeys truly do end.

In these writings, we will see the process of this journey into the Divine through the lens of this author. This journey has been influenced by the joy and sorrow of everyday living; the impact of being female and gay in a world that is not always appreciative of women and of homosexuality; my work as a political activist, an educator, social worker and psychotherapist (primarily in the fields of mental health, substance abuse, women's issues, and gay/lesbian/bisexual/transgender issues); and the spiritual process of my own psychotherapy (notice that the chapter on sorrow is significantly longer than that of joy!). Also, my writings have been significantly impacted by the wisdom of past and present mystics, various religions, as well as the teachings from the University of Creation Spirituality. It has been these lessons which have influenced me in this incredible journey called life.

In Part One, Children of the Beloved, we explore the essence of humanity as it relates to our divinity. Chapter One, *Who Are We?*, discusses our relationships with the Beloved and explores the glory of life, the joy and sorrow of existence, our ego experiences, our authentic self (divine self), the fecundity of interconnection, and our very essence which is mystical. Chapter Two, *Sense, Sensing, Sensuality*, explores life as a sensual experience, as pleasure and delight. This chapter discusses our five senses and their relationship to the human/divine connection, the sensing abilities and the chakras, and the soul of sensuality. In Chapter Three, *Sexuality and Spirituality*, we explore the dialectic of masculine and feminine; religion, sexuality, and homosexuality; compassionate sexuality and the chakras; and merging with our beloved and the Beloved.

Part Two, Connection vs. Disconnection, addresses our feelings and relationship to the Divine as well as what happens when we are disconnected from our spirit. Chapter Four, *Joy*, discusses feelings as a vital part of our humanness and how we can cultivate joy through the acceptance of all that is a part of life. Chapter Five, *The Sacredness of Sorrow*, defines depression, grief, and spiritual sorrow, and the healing properties of sorrow. Chapter Six, *Shadow and Beyond Shadow*, explores the shadow side of the personality and how unresolved shadow issues can manifest into evil behaviors and evil beings. This chapter also explores ways to heal the shadow and ways to respond to evil and embrace the grace of God.

Part Three, Being for God, expresses our need for being, not doing. As humans, we tend to always be busy, thereby denying our inner being, our source of divinity. We explore three ways to relate to the Beloved: *Nature as Blessing*, Chapter Seven; *Of Solitude and Silence*, Chapter Eight; and

Bountiful Living: Life as Prayer, Chapter Nine. All three chapters relate to the innate, inner divinity that we can manifest through listening to the guidance that is the presence of letting be.

Part Four, Doing for God, expresses our need to act on our being — to create a spiritual life through the mysticism of existence by placing it into action steps. In our doing for Goddess, we recognize that we must embrace compassion for all of life — the underlying compassion of the universe, compassion for self and for others, love of the Earth and cosmos, and union with the Beloved. This is explored in Chapter Ten, *A Mandala of Compassion*. Chapter Eleven, *Living Life as Creation and Creativity*, takes the reader through the fears of creativity into exploring the artist and the art, whether it is of work, play, relationships, or ceremony. The totality of doing for God results in *The Prophetic Call: Service and Justice-Making*, Chapter Twelve. Through our spiritual growth we begin to recognize and understand the need to be of service to the Beloved by expanding our compassion and being of service to all others.

And finally, Part Five, Union with the Beloved, explores the totality of the mysticism and prophetic call of humanity to join together as one species, one world, one thought, and one plan in order to honor our relationship with the Divine and all of his blessings. Chapter Thirteen, *Where All Our Journeys End*, summarizes this relationship between human and divine where immanence meets transcendence in a union that explodes with an orgasmic intensity of oneness.

My belief is one of panentheism — a both/and perspective that sees God in everything and everything in God. This is a holistic approach which sees life as both immanent and transcendent, of above as below, of here-and-now and beyond. When I speak of human meeting divine, please recognize that I believe the human is divine and that this expression is a way of delving into further depths (or heights) of a transcendent nature.

Within this work, you will see that a number of words are utilized to name the Absolute. Whether it is Great Spirit, Allah, the Tao, Goddess, Divine, Mother/Father, Krishna, Lord, God, Beloved, Brahman, the One, the All, Higher Power, or any other name, please utilize the name that is most comfortable for you, for we are all seeking and we all originated from the same Source. In various chapters, you will find poetry and prose created by this author, guided by the hands of the Divine. All such work is identified by italics. Also found within this work is the wisdom of so many of our mystics, both past and present. For they are the ones who guide us, teach us, and who can help to heal us if we but listen.

In darkness and in light,

immanence and transcendence,

joy and sorrow,

fear and faith,

we meet the Beloved

on the playing field of this Earth.

May you continue to meet the Beloved as you read.

Part One:

Children of the Beloved

We are all children of the Beloved for we are human beings birthed through the divinity of Goddess. As children we laugh, play, scream, run, jump, cry, sing, dance, and express joy in our very nature. This section explores the essence of humanity in our relationship with the Divine, living a sensual life, and the relationship between sexuality and spirituality.

Chapter One

WHO ARE WE?

The point of life is not to get anywhere — it is to notice that you are, and have always been, already there. You are, always and forever, in the moment of pure creation. The point of life is therefore to create — who and what you are, and then to experience that.

Neale Donald Walsch (104)

Who are we? We are the sons of Yahweh, the daughters of Goddess, the children of God, the gifts of the Divine, the blessings of the Beloved. We are the faces of our ancestors and the embodiment of our souls. We are the poetry of the Master Creator who has blessed us with the beauty, awe, and fecundity that only she can manifest. We are the music of the cosmos singing the hymns of the underlying presence of love. In all our colors, shapes and sizes, our differences and similarities, we are the joy of all eternity. For the Divine has birthed us as she has birthed all other beings in a delightful genesis of creativity. However we may define ourselves, we are first and foremost sacred beings who are here to experience who we are as co-creators in this ever-loving, ever-expanding cosmos. We were placed in this lifetime to reach our divinity through our humanity, to love one another fully and compassionately. And we do this through remembering who we are, for we are all mystics seeking to merge with the Beloved in the ultimate union with All That Is. We are spiritual beings genetically predisposed to connect to God; this is our destiny. Christian, Muslim, Jewish, Agnostic, Pagan, Buddhist, Hindu, Indigenous, Atheist, Goddess Worshipping, Taoist, Sufi — we are One.

For we have been given this beauty of life as well as the gift of thought and imagination so we might remember our oneness. What is this oneness? It is experiencing life in its totality, this love of creation and Creator. The Beloved has given us the task to be a co-creator of our own destiny, both individually and collectively. We are all imperfect perfections searching for meaning, challenged by God to find our highest selves. This is revealed through remembering and experiencing; remembering ourselves as divine beings and experiencing such divinity in our everyday lives. Our experience is in the ecstasy, pain, sorrow, excitement, pleasure, joy, and grief of living and loving, of being and doing. This is the experience that leads us to evolve as human beings and as soul manifestations seeking always to connect and to love. This is to remember who we really are — love embodied. The mystical activist, Andrew Harvey, relates:

> I believe that we are here to learn through adoration the love that moves the earth and stars. Coming to learn that love and its shining in all things opens our heart more and more to it in an ecstasy of tenderness and gratitude, until that time comes when all the sinews of our heart have been eased back and opened so wide that this entire universe and our entire experience of it can be placed within. (170)

We expand to such love by healing our souls, by healing our pain and sorrow, by seeking our authentic, divine self through the blessing and adoration of the Divine himself. For while we may wish enlightenment, it is a task that involves passion, work, acceptance, and the letting go of the false ego self. This is the task placed before us; this is what is being asked of us and for us.

Should we choose to commit to such a task, we have made the first step into the journey to God. For making a commitment demonstrates a willingness to seek our destiny; it is a pact made with the whole of eternity. And from this commitment, we launch into a spiral of transcendence which weaves in and out of each and every thought, feeling, and action. How far does this spiral take us? As far as the *love that moves the earth and stars*.

In reaching the earth and stars we return to our core of divinity which so often has been buried beneath our core of humanity. And while we seek to balance the dialectic of human/divine, we often have to wade through layers of human muck to expand into the love and compassion in which we were birthed. These layers include our attachments, addictions, half-truths and denials, physical and mental illnesses, projections, and the false egos which have been formed to try to protect us, but which, in reality, divert us from the experience of Oneness which we all seek (whether consciously or unconsciously).

We have been placed on this Earth in a human body with a human personality in order to learn who we are and why we are here. In our humanness, we experience the delights of our bodies, our minds, and our personalities, and in doing so, we remember ourselves as holy beings. This is an experience of union where the personality meets the divine. In this experience, we learn to expand beyond our individual self into the universal self. While we could remain in a narcissistic grandiosity of self pleasure, we have been given the destiny of so much more for ourselves, for others, and for the cosmos. And now is the time that we must expand beyond the narcissism for if we do not, life as we know it will cease to exist as we destroy the planet through our grandiosity of using the Earth and one another instead of being companions that coexist in a natural grace. We are in a critical time period, and in order to survive as a species on this blessed planet, we must expand our identification of ourselves from the limitedness of our human personality into the totality of the Universal All.

In order to do this, we do not have to deny ourselves our pleasures, but to redefine what is pleasurable. For pleasure is purely a subjective experience and one which can be altered from the material to the holy. And while we do not need to deny ourselves all our material goods, we seek to do no harm to ourselves, others, or to the environment as we pursue such pleasures. This comes as we let go of the false ego self and its need for "things," into the authentic self which is the pleasure of the heart and soul. And while things may still be desired, they are not material wants which rape the environment and one another.

A friend recently expressed surprise that I used to be caught up in material things. She said she considered me one of the least materialistic people she knew. But she didn't know me back in the days of narcissistic, material splendor –- splendor that was mostly desired –- although I often bought things I didn't need. My mother used to tell me I had champagne taste on a beer budget when we would go to various Parade of Homes tours and explore how the wealthy lived, and I would find extravagant homes I wished I could buy.

So when I moved to northern Michigan, I decided I had to have a boat. Having a boat in an area surrounded by water is seen as a need here, not a want. So my partner and I decided to buy a used motor boat, a small 14 foot Bayliner with an open bow. Nothing fancy, as we were living on the salaries of social workers. Now I enjoyed this toy, but it didn't change my life experience, make me happier, or complete me as an individual. But the day that I put the boat in the water after a long season of hibernation and it began to sink was the day I decided this was one material good I no longer needed. Along with me in the sinking boat was my father, a non-swimmer. As we made it safely back to shore and discovered that the plug hadn't been put back in after storage, I took it as a sign that simpler was better. Now, one of my greatest pleasures is lying on a $9.95 blow-up raft that I paddle myself for it allows me to peacefully coexist with the beauty of nature. Material pleasures are delightful, but not if they are sought to ease the soul, for the soul doesn't need such pandering. The soul only needs the authenticity of the divine truth of compassion and love.

When we explore this false ego, we discover that it is cut off from the truth –- that there is only love — the truth of the heart and the spirit. The false ego is created over time; we are not born with it. We are born only of divine love, authenticity, and truth. Even if we were conceived through trauma or were unwanted by our human parents, the Beloved celebrated our birth in love and light. Yet as we grow older, the memories of our holiness become cloudy, and we begin to create a false self in an attempt to define who we believe we are. Notice this difference: to create who we believe we are, rather than remember who we already are. And so we begin to create out of ego instead of listening to the truth of the heart. In this false creativity, we begin to define ourselves as individuals with our own wants and needs instead of as co-beings of universal oneness. This false identity lies to us, but because we have become so distant from our core selves, we take these lies as the truth, and so it begins — a path of un-authenticity. We have now created an identity of separation and in our separation, we begin to operate out of fear and scarcity. And fear and scarcity are not of Goddess, but only of the limited human personality.

I work with many people who have suffered through traumatic child-hoods: being an unwanted pregnancy; being physically, sexually, emotion-ally, and spiritually abused; being unheard. Horrific childhoods of torture, rape, and emotional deprivation. One person revealed that she was con-ceived out of hate (a rape), so how could I ever think that she was birthed out of compassion. She is a compassionate person who gives back to oth-ers. Yet she needs to learn to love herself and be loved by the Divine; no simple task, as she had created a false self to protect herself from further hurt and pain. This false self kept her inner divinity hidden behind a mask of false pride, a mask of independence instead of interdependence, and a mask of emotional numbness that she covered with her competence as a helping professional. Yet with the work in therapy and in her spiritual pro-gram, she is transforming into the divine being that she has always been.

While the ego is so often maligned in our urgency to blame something for our misbehaviors, it must be challenged and redefined into the truth-fulness of the heart. We must discover our true self, that self which is defined through the spiritual presence of the heart. Yet the heart must go through its own purification in order to heal; this is the purpose of the joy and the trauma of life. In this journey to our authentic self, we must let go of our fears and scarcity mentality and then trust that the Beloved can take us through any concern, any despair, and any horror as well as guide us in our joyfulness. This comes through love — love as the ultimate healer. Love that is the balm for all falsehoods. Love that heals the personality to its core on both individual and universal levels. Because while we have core differences, we also have a universal core, that which is the soul of the universe that resides in every one of us. For this is the true personality, the authentic self, the healthy ego. Kabir Helminski, a Sufi mystic, states that the "ego is a fundamentally positive energy with many positive qualities: aspiration, diligence, responsibility, self-respect, discipline, and integrity" (64). But only by taming the false self, the self the hides such positive energy, and by loving it to its core do we delve into our heart song — the song of Oneness.

This Oneness is of the heart, mind, and soul. It is the love of the nature of all existence that defines our very essence. It is the love that encompasses ourselves, others, nature, and the cosmos. This is the core of mysticism, for mysticism is the love beyond the human self, a transcendent love of all of existence. "Mysticism," relates Evelyn Underhill in her clas-sic text, *Mysticism*, "in its pure form, is the science of ultimates, the science of union with the Absolute, and nothing else, and that the mystic is the person who attains to this union, not the person who talks about it. Not to *know about*, but to *Be*, is the mark of the real initiate" (72).

The woman born of a rape that was mentioned above, is an example of a person becoming a mystic, although that mystical nature has always been within her. We are all mystics whether we recognize this or not, for mystery is the grandest part of our godliness. We have been created out of mystery by a Creator who is fully mysterious. This mystery is the expansion of the self into the mysterious soul of the cosmos. We carry each and every atom of the beginning of the cosmos, each and every atom that is the core of the Beloved himself. We understand that we carry the past, the present, and the future in our genetically coded scripts. These scripts define us both as individuals and as interrelated members of the Oneness of the Absolute. This is our universal oneness, this dust of eternity. We cannot escape this ultimate truth. And the Truth is love: love of self, of others, of the cosmos, and of the Goddess.

We are all mystics since we have all been touched by the Divine. These experiences may be small intimate glimpses or they may be expansive, transcendent states of union. We can explore these mystical experiences. They may occur during an expedition in nature with God's light shining upon the land and seas; or when gazing into the eyes of a child; or while creating a work of art; perhaps with the rapture of passionate, loving sex with a cherished partner; in reading spiritual texts, or in the silence of a sanctuary. Perhaps a mystical moment is occurring right now as you remember who you are. This is the awe and passion of a mystical life, this spiritual oneness. For we are our bodies and souls and we are beyond our bodies and souls. We are living, breathing, sentient beings that expand into the sensuousness of co-creativity, birthing along with our Mother of all of life. This co-creativity is giving birth to that which defines us in our joyfulness and awe, whether that creativity is raising a child, writing a song, or playing a game. This is who we are in the unity of life because separation does not exist. We are love embodied in our human form; we are co-creators with God; we are the passion of the Divine. We must celebrate this emergent immanence and transcendence — this here-and-now experience of our humanness with the mysticism of the holy. For this is who we are and why we are here.

You fill me with an exuberance of spirit,

    a joy of existence,

    a passion of orgasmic intensity.

Fill me, Oh Goddess of my desire,

    fill me solely to do thy will.

Fill me beyond my level of capacity

    so I might drown in your blessedness.

Take me to the limits of my being,

    a being that is nothing without You.

I rest in the delights

    of your supple breast

    of motherly love.

This supple breast of motherly love is a divine expression of sensuality. Sensuality which is of the human and of the Divine, which is Mystery and mysticism, expands as we expand. We explore such beauty in the expressions of our selves and of the universe. For sensuality is.

Chapter Two

SENSE, SENSING, SENSUALITY

I understood that
our sensuality is grounded
in Nature, in Compassion
and in Grace.
This enables us to receive
gifts that lead to
everlasting life.
For I saw that in our sensuality
God is.
For God is never out of
the soul. (1-11)

Julian of Norwich (Doyle 92)

Life is a sensual experience. Everything we are, everything we do, everything we *be* is steeped in sensuality. We are sentient beings in a cosmos defined by her living essence. Gaia herself is an exciting, quivering mass of ever-changing, ever-growing, ever-healing energy that collides and expands into the dynamism of the universe. As people on this planet in this cosmogenic force field, we ebb and flow to the rhythms of nature, which of course, is the rhythm of Goddess, our source of all life who is the One who is truly fully sensuous. She is always embracing, loving, and birthing in an ongoing climactic release of life energy.

To deny that the Divine is sensual is to reject the underlying essence of existence. God has birthed each and every sentient being, and each and every "non-sentient" being, although there really is no such thing as everything glows with the pulse of life, in a magnificent genesis of creation. And to deny our own sensuality is to deny Yahweh of the beauty, the expansiveness, the joy of his creation.

But what about the denial of our own sacred pleasure of sensing? So often we dishonor the gifts of our five senses as well as the gifts of our higher senses (intuition, insight, and unity with the Source). Our five senses — sight, sound, taste, smell, touch — are so often neglected in our daily activities. We ignore them, only utilizing them as an expectation, an expectation that they are there to meet our basic needs, nothing more. We take these senses for granted, seldom appreciating the vibrancy they give our lives. We don't allow ourselves to be enticed by them and we often neglect them in our pursuit to reach higher states of consciousness; they become a means only to an end. But our senses are an end to themselves for they are our immanent, earthy connection to our here-and-now reality, our gift of humanness. The Divine gifted these senses to us for a reason — for us to connect with who we are in our physicality. What are our senses but a sensual awareness of all that life is? We tap into Gaia, the cosmos, ourselves, and other beings through these senses.

Although our senses relate to our humanness, they also lead to openings at other levels of reality. If we allow our senses to fully open, we not only experience the immanent, but we also delve into the transcendent. All of our senses must be experienced to fully appreciate what God has gifted. These pleasures are to be enjoyed and treasured. Let us unwrap these delights.

SIGHT/VISION

There is a difference between sight and vision. Sight is related to the physical nature of seeing while vision extends to a deeper level of observation, sometimes on a different realm of existence. Vision allows us to view the comings and goings of the world, to take in the plethora of earthly stimuli. Vision is invaluable for the process of connecting with another individual, be it a child or adult. It allows a parent to mirror love, attention, and connection to an infant, this loving gaze which facilitates the bonding process. Vision allows us to gaze erotically at our partner, that look which conveys our sense of desire, passion, and love. It allows us to lovingly look at all of creation.

Yet how often do we gaze at the very sensuality of life itself? We so often take for granted what appears before us. Do we notice the perfection of a flower asserting its passion by growing in a crack in a sidewalk, the shadows overtaking the sunshine in the woods, the haggard lines in the face of the old man in the park? We miss so many opportunities to stop and view our world and see the divinity within. We need to honor the visual delights before us by allowing our eyes to see and experience, not screen, the scenery of our lives. This is how sight turns into vision.

In our vision we may begin to see other levels of reality. We know that the eyes have long been touted as the window to the soul. The eyes lead to the heart and to the intimate connection with another. They provide a mirror to see how loved and embraced we are by our beloved and the Beloved. And if we allow ourselves to be totally open to All That Is, our eyes will take us to incredible depths of our own psyche, to the psyche of others, and to the soul of the universe. Our vision can take us beyond today into the very depths of Creation herself. These eyes allow us to view our past and future lives, and to know and experience all of our relationships to others on every level of existence. If we fully allow ourselves to trust and love another and be fully trusted and loved by him, we may actually glimpse the soul, not only the soul of the person, but the universal soul of our oneness. All time, space, and here-and-now realities dissolve. Within that dissolving, the soul irradiates in its existence. What a blessing it is to view the soul of another; what an honor to be given such a gift. For to glimpse another's soul is a treasure bestowed by God which says, "I give you my all; I give you the divinity in me." It is Goddess stating, "Here I am in my entirety; I can offer you nothing more than my divine essence." Accept this gift for it is a treasure beyond words.

I found such depth in the eyes of one of my co-soul travelers, a friend that helped me along my spiritual path. Gazing into those eyes, I had glimpses of her in the past, the previous lives in which we were together, sometimes as friends, sometime as partners, sometimes male and other times female. These visions were microseconds in length and continually flashed upon my mind as a movie flashes upon a screen. I cannot describe in detail what I saw as they rushed by so quickly. However, for her, there were more detailed visions. When we met for the first time, she had a flash of me (as a male) going off to war and I was on my horse leaning down and kissing her goodbye. We were to be married upon my return. The next vision was one of sorrow, as she saw herself receiving word that I had been killed in the war.

At the end of my visions, I saw her as her soul, a perfect oneness with the Beloved. Within this complete oneness of vision, I felt an all-encompassing sense of unity and peace with her, the universe, and the All. And for the both of us, these experiences led us into further levels of transcendent merging. These remain some of my most treasured moments, and I sometimes call upon them to comfort and soothe me.

Let me gaze into your golden eyes.

Those eyes that have taken me to places

previously unknown.

I can see, feel, touch the entire universe

through those eyes.

They bring me to a place of peace,

of calmness, of joy, of passion,

of total connectedness.

Do you know the power of those eyes?

They bring me home time and time again.

Come home with me.

HEARING/LISTENING

In our everyday lives, we are constantly bombarded with noise and because of this, we often turn off our hearing, muting not only the noise in our lives, but shutting off the vitality of sound as well. While we may actually hear these sounds, do we really listen to them? Listening is attending to that which surrounds us. Listening allows us to connect to our everyday existence if we so allow it. But in our hearing, we often never listen — sometimes because we feel overloaded by the ongoing stimuli in our surroundings, sometimes because we are too impatient and too focused on doing that we don't bless ourselves with the gift of listening, and sometimes because we are too fearful of tuning into our inner lives to hear the whisper of silence. For silence is as much of listening as is sound, and silence is a sound like no other.

But there is a difference between noise and sound. So frequently we are bombarded with noise, noise that jars us to our very souls, noise that reaps havoc upon our psyches and our spirits, not to mention what it does to the hearing/physical aspect of our human systems. Is it no wonder that we learn to tune out the roar of an airplane taking off, the obnoxious whining of a jet ski, or the incessant ringing of the telephone?

How different this noise is from the beauty of the sound of nature — waves lapping upon the shoreline, swans honking the sounds of their souls, fall leaves rustling underneath our feet. I love where I live because I am so connected with these sounds of nature and when there is too much noise around where I live, I head to the Nature Conservancy woods and beach where there is both stillness and the sounds of nature, not the noise of boats, cars, and horns. I grew up on a farm in northern Indiana in a home that was surrounded by twelve acres of woods, and I learned as a child that this connection to nature enriches my life and is one of the ways I connect to the Beloved. In this silence of eternity, I continue to connect to all that surrounds me –- the sounds of Mother Earth displaying her soulfulness.

Yet because of this over-stimulation of noise, we often miss the plethora of healing sounds, joyful, awesome sounds, the sounds of life and living. We must begin to listen, not just hear, but listen to these sounds as they are the sounds of our soul, just as the honking of the swan is the sound of her soul. These sounds reverberate within us; we know that their very essence strikes a cord deep inside our being. Music, nature, chanting, the underlying sound of the universe, and quiet are all sounds that entice us to become one with ourselves, God, and all of the cosmos. We innately understand that these sounds touch our core and allow us to delve deeper into the vibration of the universe, the connection to All That Is.

In our hearing, we need to listen to the sound of silence. In the quiet we listen to the stories of others; this is the greatest honor we can bestow upon another. To love another so much that we provide our rapt attention, listening through our heart to allow another to fully enter us and to touch us at the level of the psyche. We are all voices of Goddess and we must listen to the words and the wisdom of such voices. All voices, the sounds of nature, other humans, angels whispering in our ears, as well as the voice of the cosmos in her sounds of life and her sounds of silence, contain the inherent wisdom of the divine universe. This is the blessing of the reverence of sound.

Years ago, I went to visit two friends. They weren't home from work so I sat in the yard listening to the sounds of silence. Then I heard this small voice which told me to go home as there were four messages on my answering machine and one was about a job. I tried to ignore this voice, telling myself there was no way I had four messages in that short of time period; plus, I had just given my resume to an agency the day before. But the need to go home was just too strong. I left a note for my friends and went on my way. When I got home, there were four messages on the machine and one of them was about a job interview. I got the job a week later.

TASTE

The pleasure of taste is an often overlooked sensation in our hectic lives in which eating and consuming are the goals, not the pleasure. In an environment in which one world is filled with overabundance and obesity, another world filled with hunger and starvation, the sense of taste is neglected in favor of filling the void — whether it is physical, emotional, or spiritual. This filling may result in overeating, anorexia, or bulimia. And for the poor and hungry, eating is simply about survival. But food and drink not only are the very nature of survival, they are providers of a sensuality of nature, the succulent delight of imbibing on tasty treats. Eating can become a sensation of pleasure, not only the taste, but the ritual of blessing what has been provided and the very ceremony of enjoying the process of eating and of tasting. To revel in the flow of the waters and the delicacies of the feast is to bask in the sustenance which has been given.

Yet taste goes beyond the taste of food; taste is a delight in other physical pleasures as well. The sensuality of the taste of another's lips, the taste of snowflakes or raindrops flavoring the Earth with a delight of Beloved's abundance, the taste of the passion of all that life is, these are the pleasures of the delicacies of life. We all need to have soul food that allows us to enter into delight — relationships with others, time alone, creative work and play — for this taste of life is a spiritual ecstasy. Whether this taste is a literal interpretation of something edible or a figurative connotation of the metaphysical meaning of life, taste is a delight provided by the senses, a sense that life is a feast to be imbibed upon. Taste is a sensual experience of life-giving pleasure.

I taste the succulent lips

dipped in honeyed lipstick,

a taste that lingers upon my psyche.

The edible delights of flavored breath,

creamy skin,

sweet sweat,

sexual flowings

tempting me beyond reason,

an insanity of ecstasy.

Treasures of your sensuality,

a plethora of delicacies sandwiches

my head.

You say: "Take, eat, this is my body."

"Oh Christ."

I devour you.

But too often this taste for life, all life, is severely neglected. The spiritual longing, if it is even acknowledged, is so often ignored in our pursuit for whatever other passions we might have that we believe will fill the emptiness — the addictions that tempt us and then devour us into the darkness. Vietnamese Buddhist Thich Nhat Hanh relates that, "So many people are hungry for spiritual food, there are so many hungry souls" (106). We must fill our own lives with the taste and the passion of a spirit-filled existence and help others to do the same.

SMELL

The sensation of smell is a most powerful sense with the strength of evoking memories long ago, perhaps lifetimes ago. Who can forget the scent of a loved one's perfume or the aroma of grandma's cooking? Scent can be present in long-held memories. It is often present after a loved one leaves us on this physical plane of life. How magical it is to catch a whiff of that person; how seductive it is in bringing back the heartfelt memory. We are deeply touched with reminiscence; we enter the past and immediately feel as though it is our present. Sometimes the scent is of the future; we recognize the smell but it holds no memory for us. And when we reach it in the future, our soul will remember its past. How wonderful are many of the scents. How fabulous it would be if we could bottle them and carry them with us to inhale whenever needed. But they come of their own accord, perhaps to soothe, perhaps to help us grieve, perhaps to warn.

Sometimes there are smells we really don't want to remember . . . in my case, pig and cow manure. Growing up on a farm where hogs were raised, we had smells that permeated our noses and our brains. One of the things I learned was to tell the difference between cow and pig manure, a gift that I still have. Of course, my father is much better at this as he can not only tell the difference between cows and pigs, but chickens, sheep, and horses . . . . Who knows when such gifts will come in handy? Who knows when my sense of smell will begin to falter and I can no longer identify manure? But if I can't smell the manure, I won't be able to smell the pleasurable aromas. Life is a dialectic.

Do we allow ourselves to bask in the scents that surround us on a daily basis? Do we let the aromas of life pleasure us? Do we imbibe in these pleasures? How often do we really stop and smell the dandelions? We must honor these scents of the Earth and her blessings — the flowers, the land, the rain, the grass, the seas, and even the manure. We need to honor the scents of our own humanness and our own passions. Smells are a delight of our immanent connection to all of life, but yet another sense that we typically ignore in our hurried lives.

The morning wind spreads its fresh smell.
We must get up and take that in,
that wind that lets us live.
Breathe before it's gone. (1-4)
                                    Rumi (Barks 267)

TOUCH

Touching and being touched, divine gifts that are so often denied because of our fears of bodily pleasure. How many of us learned early in life that to touch ourselves (especially in sexual areas) was dirty, sinful, and shameful or were denied the sensations by our caregivers because somehow, touch meant sexual touch? And how many of us were inappropriately touched through physical and sexual abuse? But we know that touch is life-giving and without it, babies develop a "failure to thrive" syndrome, a condition in which their physical and emotional development may be permanently stunted and in which they can actually die. Touch is a life force, an energy that we need not only as babies, but as adults. Just the simple expression of holding a hand, giving a hug, or patting a shoulder not only provides comfort, but also creative, life-giving essence that empowers and heals.

So often we deny ourselves and others the sensuality of the physical form of the body. We need to exalt in loving and caressing our body, gaze at its loveliness, and express gratefulness for its miraculous pulsations of life. Touching our bodies enables us to feel the physicality of life in its most sensual form. Caressing and stroking, perhaps for sensual pleasure, perhaps also for sexual pleasure, are the means of a spiritual relationship to our most immanent part of being human. Simply pleasuring ourselves through rubbing, scratching, tickling, caressing, kneading, stroking and massaging are delights of the body, spirit, and soul.

Touching also goes beyond that of touching ourselves to touching other beings and objects that provide pleasure. Stroking a cat, feeling the rough bark of a tree or the smoothness of a stone, fondling silk material, running sand through our fingers or soaking in a hot bath, are other physical sensations provided to us through the touch of Goddess herself.

When I was recovering from back surgery, my partner told me that our two cats took turns lying beside me in bed to help to comfort and heal. These two cats did not like one another, but appeared to work out a truce between them in order to help me. Pets are so wonderfully compassionate, nurturing, and loving; their very essence is healing. These cats would lie beside me so I could pet them as they knew the comfort they provided. Yet after I had recovered, they reverted to enemies, hissing, growling, and fighting one another. If only they could have found compassion between each other!

There are also the delights of pleasuring others as well. Just as we indulge in the mysteries of our own sensuality, we need to learn how to honor and enjoy the bodily sensations of others. From the warmth of a hug to the intensity of passionate sex, touch soothes the soul and allows two spirits to connect not only on the human level, but also on a transcendent level. We are biologically predisposed to this need for touch and the powerful sensations provided through stroking invoke nurturance, connection, and love; love that is of the Divine in each and every one of us.

As we have seen, if we allow the five senses their due, they not only are our immanent connection to life, but they can carry us beyond physical sensations into other realms of our being. This is the world of sensing.

SENSING AND THE CHAKRAS

Sensing is about our innate knowledge, the wisdom of all the ages and all of the ancestors, the insights and intuitions that guide us from a deeper level, a spiritual level that is opened through these five senses as well as through our chakras. Chakras are our psychic energy sources that are located in the subtle body, the astral plane that relates to the physical body. There are seven major chakras each with their own powers and perceptions, which form a pattern of life energy unique to each person. This universal life force energizes the physical, mental, emotional/psychological, and spiritual bodies of an individual.

The chakras and our senses are closely related. To open to our senses is to open to these energy centers. When we open the chakras, we fully experience all the senses on a physical and soul level. Our first three chakras reflect the physicality of life. They are called the lower chakras because of their placement on the lower half of the body. Believing that these are lower chakras of a lesser life force because they are most closely related to the physical body is to denigrate the importance of their existence. Also, while they are most closely related to the physical realm, it must be noted that each and every one has a connection to a spiritual/psychic plane.

Let's examine each chakra and see how it relates to our own functioning as we discuss a fictional psychotherapy client, Susan, age 37, who is experiencing difficulties in life. Susan has been seeking help for past trauma issues and alcoholism. She is married, has two young children (a boy, age 10; and a girl, age 7), and is trained as a nurse. She is currently working part-time at the local hospital. She has a number of hobbies and interests and has some supportive friends. However, her level of functioning has decreased since she has been having more memories and flashbacks of being raped at age 17. Along with these increased memories, she has begun to increase her intake of alcohol. Her father is a recovering alcoholic and she grew up with his drinking being denied and covered-up by her family. Susan is the younger of two children and has an older brother, Tom.

The first chakra, the root chakra, is located at the base of the spine and is the source of grounding to the Earth. It is the chakra of life and death, our connection with family and with our ancestors. It is the energy realm of basic needs, structure, and group identity. However, there is also a deeper psychic connection to the forces of the Earth and cosmos, as well as a relationship to the past through our ancestors.

Our client, Susan, is into the fire of the first chakra. She had her basic needs met in childhood, although there were some issues due to her father's drinking. She currently feels safe with her family, neighborhood, and life in general, although the rape memories are intruding upon such feelings of safety. Through therapy, she is becoming more attuned to her senses and sees how she has often ignored them as a way to numb herself from the pain. She is also examining some of her core beliefs which are at odds with her family-of-origin, especially beliefs and rules surrounding the cover-up of her father's alcoholism when she was a child. In order to ground herself to life, she has been walking in the woods surrounding her home and working in her garden. This has allowed her to become more attached to her senses and the Earth.

This chakra opens the way into our second chakra which is located around the area of the pelvis and navel. It is related to sexuality and relationships and is another one of the physical chakras, as it is about who we are as sexual beings in relationship to ourselves and to others. The second chakra is also concerned with creativity, the creativity of birth as a physical act, as well as the creative force of other births, whether they be of an idea, a piece of artwork, or a musical score. This chakra relates to the sixth chakra which expands upon this birth into a level of spiritual connection.

Susan has been experiencing intimacy problems with her husband secondary to the rape trauma memories and flashbacks she has been having. She has lost her sexual desire and has been having flashbacks of the rape during sex. Susan has been doing artwork as a way to express her creativity and as a way to work through the rape trauma. She brings the paintings to therapy in order to process her grief. She and her husband are working on basic intimacy tasks such as holding hands and massaging one another in order for Susan to help regain her trust (third chakra issues) and her connection to herself and her own body and spirit.

Moving up the body is the third chakra located in the area of the solar plexus. This energy center completes the trilogy of the physical senses and is related to issues of power, control, and self-esteem. It is the chakra of the ego and how we see ourselves within our human bodies as related to the world around us. It, too, is connected to a higher self because only through the development of a strong ego do we become capable of entering into the realm of the spirit.

Susan is struggling with self-esteem issues, again primarily related to the rape and the core messages she and society have given her regarding being a rape survivor. She is working on trust issues with her husband. However, Susan's drinking has increased as a way for her to try to cope with her self esteem and feelings of being "dirty" and violated. Drinking also gives her pseudo-power as she believes that alcohol gives her confidence. She recently began attending AA meetings and is learning that she is powerless over alcohol, but that she is powerful in her recovery.

Our next chakra is the fourth or heart chakra, which mediates between the three physical chakras and the three chakras of the spirit. All emotions are channeled through this energy vortex. The heart center is our connection of love, compassion, and passion with and for all of life. This energy center is one of healing — healing for ourselves and for others, including all of nature and the cosmos, as well as healing universally. This is the chakra that when fully opened, propels us further into a relationship with the Divine.

Susan, who by her very nature is compassionate, is continuing to open her heart and soul through meditation, prayer, massage, and artwork, and through trusting others in her life, including increasing trust with her husband. She is a nurse in pediatrics at the hospital, and this is also an outlet for her compassion. She is experiencing heart pain through grieving her losses, but is also experiencing openness to such heart experiences on a level she has never before felt.

While all of our chakras relate to our divinity, our fifth, sixth, and seventh chakras are more specifically related to our higher self, the connection with God/Goddess. The fifth chakra is located in the area of the throat and is the communication center on both physical and psychic levels; it is about speaking the truth. In speaking the truth, this center teaches us to let go of our will into Divine will. Yet we must first relate to our own sense of will and what it teaches us before we can join into the will of the Beloved.

Addiction is also an issue for the fifth chakra, and as previously noted, Susan is addressing this. This issue is addressed as Susan focuses on her recovery and her own voice regarding her trauma, grief, and alcoholism. Also, by telling her life story to her therapist, she is further connected to this chakra energy because telling her story allows her to release the shame connected to her rape and alcoholism. She is making healthier decisions for herself and using her will to do so. Susan is also connecting to the psychic level of all those who have gone before her and who have also transcended such trauma.

The sixth center is also called the third eye chakra and is located between our physical eyes. This is one of psychic connection and our perception of reality. It relates to our senses of insight, intuition, wisdom, and creativity. This chakra is a combination of our left and right brain which results in the totality of creative energies. These are divine connections expressed in human form.

Susan is discovering that by opening all of her energy centers through connecting to the Earth, therapy, art work, meditation, and massage, she is able to intuit what she must do for herself. She is able to honor the wisdom and intelligence that resides within her. She is able to see the truth of her existence instead of focusing on the shame which has overcome her. This is the creativity of healing on both immanent and transcendent levels.

Finally, the seventh energy system is the crown chakra, located at the top of the head, which is of the ultimate relationship to the One. This charka fully integrates body, mind, spirit, and soul. Caroline Myss, whose work focuses on energy medicine, states: "The seventh chakra is our connection to our spiritual nature and our capacity to allow our spirituality to become an integral part of our physical lives and guide us" (265). It integrates all that we have learned and expands this understanding into a deeper understanding, the total being of divinity.

Susan has begun to feel more connected to a Higher Source, whom she calls Goddess. She has been involved in religious practices in the past, but never felt a connection to her own innate divinity. With her openness and willingness to do the work of grieving, she has begun to develop a sense of peace and a relationship with divinity both within and without. She is developing faith that she can work through her issues and become a stronger, more compassionate woman. She is working to open and integrate all of her chakras as a way to heal from her life traumas.

The senses and the chakras are levels of earthly and spiritual connections that can expand beyond the physical self into the higher self. We can take into account not only the actual physical stimuli, but also expand into a level of sensing. Sensing is about our insights, intuitions and wisdom, and is evidence of a Higher Presence guiding our every thought and behavior.

Insight and intuition are closely related; insight is the understanding we grasp through intuition. It is the deeper connection to the inner nature of things. Intuition is information gathered without conscious thought for it is that inner wisdom of our spirit guiding us through love and light. Wisdom that is beyond human consciousness; wisdom that is of the Source who bestows us with the knowledge of the cosmos and all the ages. Scientist and philosopher Gary Zukav tells us that, "From the multisensory point of view, insights, intuitions, hunches and inspirations are messages from the soul, or from advanced intelligences that assist the soul on its

evolutionary journey" (80).   This multisensory view includes the five
senses and goes beyond these senses to include other ways of higher learning. This sensing is of our self which is our purpose for existence as we are
all here to develop an even closer relationship to God. Our human, physical self meets the divine self in our daily connections of living a sensuous
life.

These senses and sensing abilities open us to the sensuality of being
a human being in a succulent, vibrating, pulsating force field of creative
energy. It is our honor and our duty to open to these pleasures of life and
to all that they gift us, both in delight and in sorrow. We are sensual as the
Divine is sensual. Let us celebrate our being.

SENSUALITY

The soul of sensuality lies within. It lies within our bodies and our
psyches. The pure physicality of life, feeling emotions and sensations connected with our deeper soul connections of wisdom, insight, and intuition,
allow us to connect with other areas of life that are sensuous. Besides the
sensuality of the mind/body/spirit/soul connection, let us explore the underlying ground of sensuality — that of our connection with the Divine and
her creativity.

While we often believe that sensuality is about physicality, what has
birthed us in our sensuality is a Creator who is truly the ultimate in the
enchantment of life. The Beloved, who created in the totality of the birth of
existence, did so in a dramatic genesis of the universe. This energy at the
dawn of creation is to be honored for its mystical quality of time, light,
space, and creativity. The Mystery has and will always be present and her
essence was first seen in the creation of the Earth and the cosmos. There
was and is the underlying awe, passion, and creativity which forms and re-
forms the basis of the universe. For this story of creation is deeply touched
by expansiveness — the expansiveness of the overwhelming acts of creation and the beauty and ecstasy of such an origin. For birthing is the ultimate sensual act, the awesomeness of new beginning. What could be more
creative than the formation of the mountains, the singing of the songbirds,
the luminosity of Luna, the roar of the ocean? Indeed, what could be?

For Goddess has given her all in the birth of nature, from the tiniest cell
to the deepest sea, and she delights in her passion of regeneration. There is the
longing to create and re-create; there is joy as well as sorrow in what has been
created. For in birthing comes violence, a violence that must exist or creation
would not continue. Within the energy system, destruction must exist in order
to revamp and re-create life forms. Life itself would no longer exist if there
was no destruction. So while there is so much delight in creation, there is sorrow over what must die in order for expansiveness to continue. In the creative

process of healing the planet, we connect to her mystical soul by honoring her through reciprocity. This is the joy, awe, and sensuality in the communion with the Earth and the entire universe. This gift which can regenerate itself if left to the Divine's creativity, must be honored.

This creativity exists in so many forms. Birthing is not only of God and of physical birth of new life, but it is about any artistic endeavor. Everything that takes place in life is brought forth through this genesis. The formation of a sculpture, the creation of a new thought, the writing of this sentence, the raising of a child, the chorography of a dance routine, are all divine expressions. These divine expressions, these sensual creations of God, nourish and sustain us for without creativity, we will die.

Sensuality is of the mystical, psychic connections of years gone by, but that reach into today and tomorrow. Sensuality is a dramatic life force energy experienced in body and soul, mind and spirit, in this dialectic life. We need to honor our senses and our sensing abilities as we expand into the depths of life as a sensual process and always remember that the Beloved, who is fully sensual, relates to us as sensual, sentient beings.

This kiss of eternity –

I am awakened from a

deep and dark slumber.

Awakened by the kiss of my Beloved;

she waits at every corner of my

innermost secrets

with the patience of Job

and the fire of eternity.

Awaiting my awakening.

This kiss frees the bliss of

Evermore.

And as we relate as sensual beings, so also do we relate as sexual beings that are also spiritual beings. For sexuality and spirituality are divinely related, as we will see in our next chapter. Such are the characteristics of the children of Goddess.

Chapter Three

SEXUALITY AND SPIRITUALITY

They try to say what are you, spiritual or sexual?

They wonder about Solomon and all his wives.

In the body of the world, they say, there is a soul

and you are that.

But we have ways within each other

that will never be said by anyone. (1-6)

Rumi (Barks, *Essential* 37)

Sexuality and spirituality — a both/and relationship that has so often been split into a duality. While it is possible to have a sexual relationship that isn't spiritual, it is impossible to be a spiritual being without a level of sexuality. Here, we need to define sexuality. Sexuality is not just about the physical act of sex (although it can be); a truly sexual being is one who embraces the intimacy, the creativity, the longing and eros, and the oneness of connection with life. These are the descriptions of a spiritual being as well. One can be celibate and still be a sexual being; one can be chaste and still be a sexual being.

When I was writing this book, I chose not to date or become involved in a relationship because I understood that my passion and sensuality needed to be channeled towards my project. I couldn't give both a relationship and the manuscript my full attention as I felt one would distract me from the other. I believe that this decision resulted in a stronger piece of writing (and I didn't drive a partner crazy as I was writing it). This writing was my birthing.

There are many activities that are sensual, where a level of ecstasy is achieved. Creativity — the birth of an idea, a piece of art work, music, close friendship, a connection to nature — whatever the process of creation, is a form of longing of the soul. Psychologist and theologian Thomas Moore comments, "Living a full sensuous life with friends, intimates, and things, and indulging in pleasurable activities is an erotic life, and it may well fulfill whatever sexual needs the soul has at a particular time" (184-185).

This level of sensuousness is our spiritual/sexual connection. It is our joy in our reverence of life. Whether we are sexual with another human being or with ourselves, whether we choose to be celibate or are chaste, or whether we are heterosexual, bisexual or homosexual, our sexuality is divinely appointed.

MASCULINE/FEMININE

We cannot explore sexuality without beginning to explore the masculine and the feminine. Psychological research has shown us that the healthy individual incorporates the positive traits traditionally associated with each sex; masculine characteristics which include a focus on cognitive skills, task orientation, independence, assertiveness, and ambition; feminine traits such as interdependence, nurturance, utilizing feelings and intuition, and being compassionate. Although this may seem to be a type of gender stereotyping, it is only meant to be utilized as a manageable framework. While we can look at femininity and masculinity on a continuum, it makes more sense to embrace this as a oneness, a unity of these energetic forces which lead to a healthy individual, an individual seeking self-actualization. For if we are in unity, there is no separation of masculine and feminine energies. Yet we still divide gender and focus on separation instead of focusing on such unity.

In the past as well as currently, the oneness of our sexuality has been subverted by patriarchal society, including religious institutions. A misogynistic attitude has pervaded our very souls and, quite obviously, affects the expression of our sexual/spiritual self. Various religions including Christianity, Buddhism, Judaism, and Islam have ignored the sacredness of the feminine — the compassion, the nurturing, and the fecundity of the divine feminine — and have been focused on the patriarchal, hierarchical systems whose control and power drove out the Goddess religions and indigenous practices. So how do we describe the healthy masculine/feminine individual? By exploring the yin and the yang, by recognizing there truly is no division for there is masculine within the feminine and feminine within the masculine. These free-flowing energies create a healthy exchange of the power of the unity. Without this powerful exchange, growth is stifled and the dialectic of an individual is lost.

For example, if a male only focuses on his masculine energy, half of the energy source is neglected (the feminine energy), leaving him depleted from the rest of the energy mass and the creativity provided by the Source. Because he is out of balance, his system attempts to reach homeostasis by connecting with someone who has the feminine energy force (and who is equally unbalanced in his or her own sexuality). This leads to an unhealthy alliance where two individuals, each shut off from half of their energy source, attempt to complement one another in a relationship; in essence, hoping that a combination of two halves make a whole — a complete energy system of the feminine/masculine. Unfortunately, what happens is that these two people are now dependent upon one another for part of their creative forces instead of having that free-flowing energy exchange within themselves and within the relationship. The result is that the relationship becomes dependent and neither individual is able to achieve wholeness alone. They may think that they have created a healthy relationship, but their relationship will begin to deplete their individual energies in order to try and maintain the partnership. In this instance, the myth of a healthy relationship has been created.

Yet for individuals who connect out of non-duality and wholeness, when two people are open to the masculine/feminine energy flow within themselves, not only are these individuals furthering their own process toward self-actualization, but they are also furthering this process for the other person as well as for the relationship itself. The relationship thrives when these two people have an even flow of creativity within and between them. The partnership then takes on another dimension — the power of the third — two whole individuals and the relationship itself. And within these three relationships is the power and the connection of the Divine, the entire completeness of creativity/creation. And when the strength of the three connects on this level, the force of the sexual-spiritual energy becomes even more energizing.

I cannot properly express the sensuality, the wonder, and the oneness that goes along with such a connection. It is beyond naming, it is beyond feeling, and it is a complete merging in which the Divine is present and sanctifies such oneness. I have experienced such completeness with one other woman in my life and the totality of such merging is the most incredible experience, for it is a human experience blessed by the desire of the Beloved.

You are the Beloved manifest.

The Beloved and I are one.

Behold me in my quest for union.

I behold the Goddess in you.

Blessed be.

So how can we honor these sacred energies? By looking at them not as separate, but as both/and and by focusing on the growth and healing potential of each and every person. For this is our divine connection to ourselves and to others. If we do not embrace this connection, our sexuality, our spirituality, our spirits, and our souls become static. The most joyful part of ourselves is shut off. How then could we expect to embrace the non-duality of sexuality/spiritually?

RELIGION, SEXUALITY, AND HOMOSEXUALITY

Traditionally, and too often currently, sexuality and spirituality have been treated as dualities — beginning and ending with the religious community. Churches have attempted, and succeeded, in keeping the populace from understanding and experiencing a sexually-based spirituality in order to control this populace. Allowing individuals to experience a transcendent state for any reason, a state that only a few chosen individuals were to achieve, would have meant that the "commoner" could become intimately connected to God, and this would not be tolerated. Because if everyone could be divinely connected, religion and thereby, religious institutions, would lose their power over the masses. Losing power and control would sabotage their worldly dominance. A fear-based mentality was instilled and unfortunately, this scare tactic continues to exist in many of our religious institutions, as evidenced by various churches' stances on issues of abortion, sex out of wedlock, masturbation, homosexuality, birth control, attitudes relative to a woman's place in the church (and society), and the inability of priests to marry. If such dictates are violated, hell and damnation result. And while the Catholic Church has led the way in such control of sexuality, numerous other churches have incorporated such beliefs into their own systems, again utilizing a body-hating, sexuality-fearing mentality.

In their work, *Coming Out of Shame: Transforming Gay and Lesbian Lives*, Kaufman and Raphael discuss how societies have suppressed sexuality, and how this suppression results in misogyny, homophobia, and hatred of our bodies, our gender, our sex, and our sexuality. And while sexuality and spirituality have been separated entities, specific expressions of sexuality are even less tolerated. This may include the so-called sins of masturbation, premarital sex, and especially homosexuality and bisexuality.

Homosexuality and *bisexuality* — two words that often instill fear not only in individuals, but in institutions. How much hate have our religious institutions perpetrated throughout the years regarding this aspect of our sexuality? How much judgment has been inflicted and at what cost? The cost of creating a fear-based mentality, the cost of human spirit, and all too often, the cost of human lives. And for what purpose? By keeping people fear-based, as already discussed, the "powers that be" have an element of control over the masses. For there must be those individuals who are "one down," marginalized groups that the majority can control. Control allows us to feel better about ourselves; the thinking becomes that of "us versus them." In the end, however, this fear (and control) allows us to stay disconnected from our spirit and our soul and keeps us from connecting with our core, the basis of love and humanity. Kaufman and Raphael express this quite succinctly:

> What most religions consider natural is heterosexual marriage; anything else is judged unnatural. If we are unnatural, we are unworthy of belonging. If we are unnatural, we oppose Nature's way and Nature's God. To be unnatural, therefore, is to be abhorrent and shameful, completely outside the natural world and the divine order of things. (89)

And what about sexuality? Do not our psychiatrists, psychologists, social workers, therapists, and researchers show us that sexuality is an orientation, a biological predisposition? Do we not know that sexuality is on a continuum —while some people may seem to be 100% heterosexual, some 100% homosexual, many of us fall somewhere in the continuum between these? And have we not yet learned that sexuality does not remain static? That someone who has been heterosexual in her sexual interactions for 20 years may now find herself in a homosexual relationship?

I have a friend who characterized himself as heterosexual for the first 50 years of his life. He married, raised a family, did all the "daddy" duties and enjoyed his life –- until he realized he was having an attraction to another man. He acted on this relationship, realizing that there had been something missing in his life — the love and companionship of a man. He now sees himself as a gay man, but believes his sexuality is fluid, as he had been married and attracted to women in the past. Nature or nurture? Perhaps both.

Religion has perpetrated and perpetuated shame in a number of areas, none more glaring than in the realm of sexuality. While we look to our religious organizations to help us open our hearts to compassion, to help us cope with our sins (sin as defined as being something that goes against our integrity as well as violates God's order), and to comfort us in times of need, we see that some churches have fueled hatred and shame. And while some churches preach tolerance, tolerance is not enough. Tolerance is merely non-hate; it is not open and loving acceptance. Tolerance is about judgment.

What must happen in religious institutions is to move beyond mere tolerance to openly embracing sexuality. Acceptance is about loving, caring, and compassion. It is about opening our hearts to the divinity within which is all-encompassing, all-embracing love. Until our institutions set such a role model of societal standards, hate and the lesser evil, tolerance, will continue to dominate.

Sexuality in general and homosexuality more specifically, have been bastardized as sins of the flesh. But our sexuality takes us to our very essence; it is a piece of the divine energy. To downplay our sexual selves and to subvert our passion is to crush the spirit. What can be more spirit-filled than loving someone to her core through our own? Whether we are heterosexual, bisexual or homosexual is not the question. The question is do we love one another openly, honestly, and totally?

Yet how difficult it is to love someone openly and honestly when openness and honesty can lead to scorn and ridicule, cause us to lose our family and friends, our jobs, our homes, and place us in a "one down" position where we can be marginalized by the masses. But for those of us who are gay/lesbian/bisexual/transgender (GLBT), our salvation is to not only embrace ourselves, but also to show others what a truly loving, spirit-filled sexuality is about. Because who can know more about love than a person who has been gay-bashed and who continues to embrace this love? We often have to endure so much in order to just love, simply love, another human being. And to put our spirit and our lives on the line is to embrace the totality of a divine relationship.

We often risk so much, for our very existence frightens and horrifies some people and various institutions. Because of this, we are more vulnerable to hate and to hate crimes, discrimination, and prejudice. We have over 1,000 fewer laws that protect us than ones that protect heterosexuals, solely because of their status of an acceptable sexuality.

Like many of us who are GLBT, I have risked being ostracized by family and friends, patronized and condemned by religious institutions, and being fired from my work if I was found out (I changed careers from teaching secondary school to that of social work as I knew I would be more openly received in the social work field). I have been refused a volunteer position working with adolescents solely due to my sexuality and was released from a volunteer position at a so-called Christian-based social service agency when a local minister told the director I was lesbian. I have lost relationships with women who couldn't cope with society's damnation of homosexual love, and been denied the legal right to marry and receive all the rights and benefits that come with this union. I watched friends who were ostracized from the medical decisions and funerals of life-partners, and who lost material goods and keepsakes to the hateful family members of the deceased partner. I have been yelled at, sworn at, and given hateful gestures due to my sexuality. I sat through a local City Commission meeting where the discussion was on local gay rights and listened to one of our esteemed leaders compare gay issues to the procreative abilities of farm animals -- "A goose needs a gander and a gander needs a goose." I had shaving cream sprayed in my mailbox and rocks thrown into my yard during a local gay rights campaign. My car was keyed because of my political beliefs.

But my challenges have been minimal compared to those who have lost families, careers, and suffered severe hate crimes. We need only look at the Matthew Shepard story, the young man who was brutally beaten and left to die tied to a fence post in a field in Wyoming, to see that compassion is missing in the sexuality/spirituality relationship. Yet we must go on and show the love that exists in such relationships. We are here to be our compassionate selves and to teach others to find their own levels of compassion beyond the prejudices.

Come meet me on the other side,

Where time stands still.

Where illusions are only illusions

And pain heals.

Come meet me on the other side,

Where love is all that matters.

Where you are free to be

- yourself

- in love

- with a woman.

With no questions asked;

And all is accepted,

Including us.

Where time stands still.

I will meet you there.

COMPASSIONATE SEXUALITY AND THE CHAKRAS

Ultimately, sexuality is about compassion; it is about loving and honoring ourselves, and it is about loving and honoring another being to the essence of her core. Compassionate sexuality is trusting oneself, trusting the other, trusting the process and honoring the divinity in one other. However, too often sex is only the physical manifestation of lust. While lust certainly has its time and place and can be passionate, it is not a compassionate expression. It is merely an act of physical release, a domination of the other, a narcissistic exercise in getting one's physical and ego needs met. But if we're healthy enough, sex is a heart experience, where physical and emotional needs are both met. Where we have the experience of loving and caring about someone else and their needs as well as our own; where compassion equals passion and passion equals compassion.

Our sexuality is experienced through our second chakra. This sexual energy can be experienced as lust, or it can become compassionate. Lust is that feeling of a purely physical state while compassionate sexuality is the entire connection of body, mind, and spirit, a sensuality that encompasses our entire being. It can be a heartfelt connection that in its ecstasy combines the force of sexuality with the force of divinity.

But in order for our sexual interactions to reach the full potential of love and compassion and then to reach to even higher levels of mysticism, the fourth and seventh chakras need to be fully open as well (While recognizing that all of these energy centers need to be open for these experiences, the second, fourth, and seventh are the most involved in the sexual/spiritual process). Although this sexual force is based in the second chakra, the transcendent state it culminates in is based in the seventh chakra, our connection to the Divine. And it cannot arrive there without first going through the mediation of the heart chakra. Remember that our first three chakras are more related to the physicality of life, while five through seven are about our spirit and connecting to our Source. The heart chakra mediates these levels through our emotions, including love and compassion. So in order for the second chakra to realize its full potential, there needs to be the heart connection (fourth) and then a Divine connection (seventh).

The fourth chakra is our feeling level connection, feelings of and for ourselves, feelings for others, our connection in spirit with another spirit. It is the main center of our emotions where compassion fully arises. The heart chakra reveals the very essence of a being, the ability to be open to joy and connection, the ability to experience the full human self. We attach to one another, to life itself, through our fourth chakra. When we combine the openness of the second and fourth chakras, our sexual connection results in a heart-felt, all-embracing union with the other. It is the power of passion. It is the power of the Divine.

There is a further path in joining sexually and that path takes the divine connection of love one step beyond. This is the experience of merging completely with another human being and with God/Goddess. Our seventh chakra is our most intimate spiritual relationship and this force connects all of our chakras and allows us, in the sexual realm (as well as in all other realms of existence), to go beyond. To go beyond our ego, to go beyond to that place of total oneness with the Source, to go beyond and transcend to the level of the Light. It is a feeling of an altered state of consciousness, a complete and total union with Yahweh and with the partner. The best way to describe this transcendence is to identify what it means to merge. There is nothing more incredible than merging with the Beloved through another human being. This melting, this glorious union, is beyond time and space.

MERGING

Let us begin in exploring the concept of merging by looking at the relationship between a human being (Rumi) and a human being who had transcended the human relationship into one filled with the Beloved (Shams). When listening or reading the poetry of Sufi poet Rumi, one cannot help but begin to understand what it is to love so intimately, so completely, so adoringly. This transcendent state is nothing more than the total loss of one's self into Divine love. Rumi achieved this level of bliss, this merging, through his love of another human being, Shams of Tabriz. Shams was Rumi's heart, soul, and mystical lover. Their story is one of love and devotion, not just to each other, but to the Beloved. Coleman Barks writes, "A doorway to eternity flickered open . . . and in one pure outrageous act of faith, Rumi dove through. In an instant of mystical annihilation, fire met fire, ocean ocean, and Rumi fell into pure being. Later he would say, 'What I once thought of as God I met today as a human being'" (*Illuminated* 7). Their story is one that transcends what we think of as human love, for Rumi and Shams related to each other on a higher plane of existence where love is not only immanent, but transcendent. Shams, the disheveled, wandering Dervish monk, had been looking for a soul such as Rumi to teach the ways of mysticism. Rumi provided such a soul and was transformed in body, mind, and spirit. They were together for a few years relating in mystical transcendence, and when Shams left and was later found dead, Rumi passionately grieved his loss. But he realized that Shams was still within him, and he began to sing, tell poetry, and dance for his love of Shams. Explore the words of Rumi and you will be forever blessed in the knowledge and the light of transcendent love.

So how do we reach this mystical state of union with the Beloved? Not through possession, but through devotion. Not through what we think of as a normal human relationship, but by giving up that perception and embracing the mystery of the gift of total oneness. A letting go of the ego, letting go of the boundaries between you and me and allowing oneself to not fall in love, but be in love; total being — no boundaries, no egos, no illusions — just a complete merging of two souls who are devoted to one another and to the Source.

Sometimes I don't know for whom I'm writing.

Is it you, the human that I love so much;

Is it the Divine that I want to connect to intimately?

Or is it the Divine in you —

A complete picture of the essence of God,

Within the human that I love?

Yet the ego plays an important role in this level of oneness. We must let the ego go and bless it on its journey so that merging can come about. But how difficult it is to let go of the ego, and in order to do so, one must have a strong, healthy ego to begin with. Without it, the merging becomes so overwhelming, so powerful, so all-connected, that fear enters and disrupts the poetry of this sacred connection; fear about losing one's identity, one's personhood, one's sense of self to another human being. The unhealthy ego responds by feeling threatened for its very existence and holds back this all-embracing union. The person without the ego strength cannot allow the merging to happen because to let go totally may feel like a total annihilation of the self. There is no sense that while the Divine embraces this level of total oneness, she also embraces the level of separateness. Because for most of us, after the merging, we eventually separate from the oneness with the other and continue to function within the individual identity (and remembering, however, that those who have achieved the highest level of transcendence will remain in such merging as a Unity, where the individual identity is obliterated). Whereas the individual with a strong, healthy ego can merge and then separate, the individual who has little sense of self can become lost in the union and feel as though she may never get out. She doesn't remember that Beloved is the totality of the union, not the other individual.

In my relationship, my partner both craved and feared this connection. We both found this level of transcendence to be a mystical experience neither of us had previously experienced and one that was life-defining and life-enhancing. Yet this total merging of our souls frightened her as she was fearful she would lose her identity and her individuality in such merging. For myself, I recognized I could be a part of such union, such oneness, and also maintain my separate identity. It was my being blessed by both the immanence and the transcendence; it was a blessing not to be taken lightly. How I have missed such union since being a single woman.

But the soul is not the one that struggles with this connection. It is the "normal" human being who experiences confusion — confusion as to the reality of the embrace of total consecrated love (the illuminated rarely experience such confusion). The human intellect wants to place the experience in a literal, concrete framework, something that makes sense to the intellect. But the soul doesn't operate out of intellect. It operates out of the heart and out of something beyond: the mystical. Who can put into an intellectual framework what this experience means? It cannot be done. And so, the person who utilizes the intellect, who doesn't go beyond the linear into a time/space continuum, who tries to make the experience rational, finds himself in a state of confusion. If he opens up and begins listening to his heart, the experience begins to have meaning outside of the rational. And once the heart is open, the Beloved enters and provides another level of understanding. Rumi states, "Stop the words now. / Open the window in the center of your (heart) [. . .]." Stop the intellect, open yourself through your heart and go beyond. "Stop the words now. / Open the window in the center of your (heart), / and let the spirits fly in and out" (21- 23) (Barks, *Essential* 35). Let the Source enter you; it is a magical experience.

If one has the ego strength to allow total annihilation of the self, to totally merge into another individual and ultimately, into Allah, then one is able to experience the most exquisite joys in life. While connecting with the Light is always a feast of love, connecting with the Divine through another human being adds another dimension. This union of two divine expressions of Goddess is beautifully described by theologian Matthew Fox who states:

> The Cosmic Christ might speak thus on the topic of sexuality: "Let religion and the churches abandon their efforts to be 'houses of sublimation.' Instead, reenter the cosmic mystery that sexuality is and teach your people, young and old, to do the same, remembering justice, remembering responsibility as intrinsic to the mystical experience. All lovemaking (as distinct from 'having sex') is Christ meeting Christ. Love beds are altars. People are temples encountering temples, the holy of holies receiving the holy of holies. Wings of cherubim and

seraphim beat to the groans and passions of human lovers, for
the cosmic powers are there eager to enhance the celebration"
(177).

This level of passion is a release of our physical self into the depth of
our spiritual self. It is an explosion of the heart and soul connection with
another heart and soul. It is the rapture of our melding with another into
eternity — eternity which is the Light of the Divine. The Divine created
sexuality for a reason. The passion, the joy, the awe and the ecstasy, the
total union with another person is the ultimate expression of human love as
consecrated in the union with the Beloved. This magical experience is
beyond time and space.

So do we continue to believe hundreds of years of religious dogma or
do we go directly to the Source and connect with what is true for our own
soul? Can the Divine, who has created sexuality, not fully embrace this
sexuality? How can All That Is not rejoice in such beautiful creation? She
cannot. For the Beloved embraces all sentient beings and their expressions
of spirituality through their sexuality.

This creation of love transcends the heterosexual-homosexual continuum. It transcends how we are wired biologically regarding sexuality. How
does it do this? By going beyond the realm of human existence into the
realm of the mystical. The Source does not care about whom we love, but
only how we love. *Homosexual, bisexual, heterosexual* are mere words that
try to define us. Divine love does not concern itself with such arbitrary definitions. Divine love only concerns itself with the essence of the love itself.

We understand that the soul takes on a life of its own regarding relationships and sexuality. The soul knows another instinctively with just a
glance. There is an incredible heart-felt connection, and a deeper love, the
soul love, that encompasses this level. Time, person, place, sex, life situations, and commitments — these have a different meaning to the soul. The
soul has its own eyes and heart which see, feel, and connect with the divinity in another. There is no ego involved, inhibitions are subverted, and the
mystery of the connection has begun. When we experience this divinity,
nothing else matters, yet we must take into account our own moral ethics
and be responsible for our desires and our actions and not act out of a self-
serving narcissism regarding such connection. For, as Thomas Moore
notes:

We might take care not to act on our desires prematurely,
because we may not yet know where they belong in the content
of our lives, but we can trust that in their depth lies the secret of
our ultimate fulfillment. They are the seeds of the soul's sexuality, somehow sorted out among our earthly lovers and the
mysterious partners known only to the soul. (239)

You are my mystical lover.

You, who permeate my very existence,

a continual bombardment upon my psyche,

a continual opening of my heart.

Eros.

Although you have left my physical presence,

your soul manifestation remains.

It is here that we continue to journey.

Your smell, your taste, your touch,

burnish me as though we just parted.

Reality - we haven't parted,

- we remain lovers in our transcendence.

In the end, what brings us home is love, Divine love — Divine love for ourselves, for every sentient being, and for the Goddess herself. There is only the totality of the embrace from God. The sheer joy of committing to another on the human level through spirit as well as on the level of the transcendent is why our Creator created sexuality. This totality is the ultimate expression of our humanity through our divinity. To deny our spirit is to deny ourselves; to deny ourselves of *what is* means to shrivel up and die, at least on a spiritual level, if not on an emotional and physical level as well. We can responsibly embrace our physicality, our emotionality, our sexuality, and our spirituality as the divinized beings that we are.

And as Children of the Beloved, with all our perfections and imperfections, we have a choice in how we respond to others and to the world around us. We can choose to connect on a spiritual level or we can choose to disconnect. How we respond is addressed in our next three chapters.

Part Two:

Connection vs. Disconnection

Through our human/divine selves, we have been given free will, and therefore, choices regarding the paths we accept in this lifetime. Part Two explores how we can become connected or disconnected from Spirit in our states of joy and sorrow as well as through the shadow side of the personality. We will also explore evil deeds and evil beings.

Chapter Four

JOY

Joy *is* the soul. The soul is that which you would call joy. Pure joy. Endless joy.

Unadulterated, unlimited, unrestricted joy. That is the *nature* of the soul.

A smile is a window to your soul. Laughter is the door.

Your heart is the corridor between your soul and your mind. The joy in your soul must move through your heart, otherwise it will "not even enter your mind."
Feelings are the language of the soul.

Joy is life, expressing. The free flow of life energy is what you call joy. The essence of life is Oneness — unity with All That Is. This is what life is: unity, *expressing*. The feeling of unity is the feeling that you call love. Therefore, in your language, it is said that the essence of life is love. Joy, then, is love, expressing freely.

Neale Donald Walsch (263-264)

What is joy but that connection to life, all of life, in a complete manifestation of oneness, a complete acceptance of what is — be it of pain or of happiness. For joy is the deepest state of feeling; it is a knowingness, an inner peace, a bliss that is ever present. Joy is about passion, the passion of life and all it offers. Passion that is of the Beloved, passion that is of the deep and abiding love of this incredible creation and all of its beings. Passion that has developed out of anguish and suffering. Passion that is the intense feeling of abiding love which is expressed through joy.

We are sentient, sensual beings who expand ourselves through honoring our feelings. We are also divine beings who delve deep within ourselves to a place of that total being — a being of joy. This is the feeling of the soul, this joy of unity. For in our joy we are passionate; in our joy we are loving and compassionate. This is the joy that we are all programmed for if we but learn to accept life as life is.

Feelings come and go — we are happy, sad, hurt, angry, frustrated, excited, bored — and these feelings are related to the meaning we place on the situations in our lives. They are transient; we may be happy one minute, angry the next. Feelings are neither good nor bad and they are there to express our humanity. Feelings are the barometers of our everyday existence. Yet we must be careful to not let our feelings dominate us as we are of our emotions and beyond our emotions, for we are also intellectual and spiritual beings. Feelings allow us to be alive, fully human, and to express our passion for life and living. Out of these feelings, out of our sensual experiences, we learn to grow into joyfulness.

For joy is a deeper level of feeling, that level of love, passion, and compassion that is of the soul. In our joy, we connect to the root of the soul, for joy is solidly grounded within the Divine. Joy embraces all feelings, all experiences, and all nuances of life. It celebrates the light as well as the dark. As Buddhist teacher Pema Chodron tells us:

Whether it's connecting with the genuine heart of sadness and the messy areas of our lives or connecting with vision and expansion and openness, what's real is all included in well-being; it's all included in joy. Joy is not about pleasure as opposed to pain and cheerfulness as opposed to sadness. Joy includes everything. (*Start* 63)

When we live life as joy, we are truly expanding our heart and soul. In such joy, we recognize life as beauty, as awe, and as creation. We connect to the interrelatedness of the living and the dying and we understand that a complete life is one of love as expressed through joy. Joy knows no boundaries for it weaves in and around all of existence. We were birthed in joy (although painfully so) and when we leave this physical plane at death, we will return to our origins in joy.

Joy is also about the human spirit. It is that overwhelming feeling that life is to be lived and experienced to the fullest. While we may confuse happiness with joy, there is a difference. Happiness tends to be transient; it flows out of having good things happen to us. It is so very easy to be happy when things are going well in life — when the marriage is good, the job is exciting, the stock market and our investments are strong, the kids are well-behaved and doing well in school, the cat is content. But where is happiness when the marriage fails, we're fired from work, the stock market crashes, the kids are flunking out and into drugs, and the cat dies? This then, is where we seek our joy, our deeper connection to the life and spirit of our being.

For it is our spirit that keeps our soul flying into eternity. It is our spirit that takes heart and lives life to the fullest. The spirit is our joy at being alive through the good and the bad times. Nothing better exudes such joy than the television show *M.A.S.H.* No matter how many episodes I watch of the same show, I can still laugh hysterically and cry in sorrow as well as in joy. For this show captures the human spirit — the delight of living behind everyday trauma and sorrow. This show continues to have much to teach us about living and dying joyfully.

Underlying joy is wisdom and gratefulness. Wisdom is the understanding that no matter what happens to us on a human level, all is well, for we are life and love as created by heaven and Earth. This is the wisdom of all the ages, the wisdom of the ancestors, the wisdom of the Beloved. For wisdom is that which surpasses all understanding as it is gathered from the divinity within and without.

Joy also springs forth from gratefulness; this is blessing and being blessed. For gratefulness is our fullest expression of divinity. Only in our acceptance of life as life is can we find joy. We must learn gratitude first, and then our joy will come. However, we tend to have this backwards as we believe we feel joy and then become grateful. Yes, we can be grateful for our joy, but we must also allow our joy to spring forth from our gratefulness. This is a deeper joy for we are not allowing our joy to be dependent upon situations, events, people, things, feelings, or anything external, but only upon the desire for what is and what will be. This is our connection to divinity, to the soul of our very being. This is the joy of acceptance, this underlying force of goodness and gratefulness that teaches us to embrace what has been given. If we embrace what is in any given situation, we find that every situation is a blessing.

Such gratefulness was found in the lessons I learned in letting go of a significant person in my life. While there was pain in the ending of this relationship, there was also the transformation that resulted — a joy of understanding what was gained and what was lost. What was lost was the person who allowed me to go into such transcendence with love and joy; what was gained was the intimacy and transcendence of a spirit-filled relationship that allowed me to grow along my path of spiritual emergence. This was a letting go and letting be experience and a journey of trusting the process, and while this relationship was not meant to last forever in this lifetime, perhaps it will be once again in another place and time. This was a relationship of heart-felt connections and growth of spirit and one that allowed me to go on with my life and return to school, write this book, and immerse myself in the silence and the peace, and in the gratitude and joy of living.

What is such joy? Joy is the sound of crackling wood in the fireplace, making angels in the snow, working out a conflict with a loved one, watching your cat sleep, grieving the death of a child, singing in the shower, ending a relationship, starting a new relationship, praying for peace, eating ice cream, raking fall leaves, stubbing your toe, reading a mystery novel, venting your anger, weeping during a sad movie, throwing a frisbee to your dog, imbibing upon decadent dessert, being fired from a job, soaking in a hot tub, lighting candles, meditating, wind surfing, holding a funeral for a pet, falling in love, laughing with friends.

For true joy is expressed by the person who has lost everything and still loves life. Because joy is our connection to divinity through our humanity — nothing more, nothing less. One who can suffer the death of a loved one, the loss of material wealth, the trauma of a divorce, the terror of a bombing — who can still embrace life within all of its pain — is a person who understands the meaning and the purpose of joy. Joy is our flying into the beauty of life; joy is wisdom and gratitude; joy is passion and compassion. Joy is.

A friend of mine lost her adult daughter to suicide. Besides the trauma of the death, there was also the added trauma of this being death by suicide, which is so much more traumatic to the survivors as the questions are, "What did I do wrong? What could I have done? Is it my fault?" But I watched my friend go through this process and heal from it. She took something horrific and found joy in what this relationship had been and joy in being able to go on and not only survive this loss, but transform and grow spiritually through this. She did this through grieving with friends, family, and a therapist; through prayer and meditation; through accepting her loss and being grateful for what this child had brought into her life; and through trusting that God was there in the darkness and would show her the Light. She also allowed her heart to tear apart and then to heal into further compassion and love. For how we handle our grief is how we heal through our everyday wounds and sorrows.

How do we cultivate such joy? As already mentioned, we do so by being grateful, by recognizing life as blessing and honoring such blessing. In our blessing, we praise and revere life as life is. This is an acceptance for all that has been given as well as all that we perceive that has not been given or has been lost. For joy only comes upon those who accept both the gifts and the limitations of life; who are grateful for the sun and the clouds, the pain and the delight, the fullness and the emptiness. This is the joy that cannot be denied for it is steeped in the blessing of divinity.

Pema Chodron states that we cultivate joy by staying in the present, by being "fully connected with the moment, paying attention to the details of ordinary life" (*Places* 62). This is staying conscious — being aware of who and what we are in our everyday existence. Relating to everything in the moment and practicing mindfulness. For when we are fully present, fully in the now, we cannot but feel joy for this second, this time, this presence. This is the gift of ordinary life.

In our consciousness, we also expand beyond the false ego into the authentic ego, that of our divine nature. We tap the essence of our higher self, the goodness of our being, and recognize that even if our human situation appears disordered, all is in divine order. In our authenticity we nurture compassion, interrelatedness, and love. We recognize that there is suffering and we work to relieve not only our own suffering, but the suffering of all sentient beings including the planet. For compassion takes us out of our narcissistic concerns into the concerns of the greater good and we grow with such compassion. The Dalai Lama notes that, "The highest happiness {i.e., joy} is when one reaches the stage of Liberation, at which there is no more suffering. That's genuine, lasting happiness. True happiness relates more to the mind and heart" (33). Pain is an everyday occurrence, but suffering is allowing the pain to control our lives, and our highest happiness is that joy beyond suffering. I've always liked the saying, "Pain is inevitable, suffering is optional." For suffering keeps us wallowing in the pain, not allowing us to heal beyond such pain.

Yet perhaps the most difficult component of nurturing joy is that of changing our thinking, of letting go of negative mental states and focusing on the positives. For our thoughts must be balanced with our emotions and our spirits. If not, our thinking can become disordered and if left unfettered, can run rampant in our lives, providing us with false information which leads to fear, not joy. This then, can be overcome by reframing our difficulties into learning experiences, growth experiences. Utilizing affirmations, allowing ourselves to feel, delving into the depths of the soul, and focusing on strengths and on goodness, allows us to transform into higher levels of thinking and of being.

A friend of mine suffered horrible abuse as a child. Locked in closets, beaten with a belt, sexually abused by her father and brother as a young child until teenage years, abandoned by her mother who didn't intervene in the abuse, she is a true survivor. She is also a person filled with joy. I remember taking one of those insipid quizzes in a women's magazine with her. It was about happiness and you rated on a scale of -5 to +5 your happiness level to various questions. Her total score was that of high happiness and I expressed my amazement that she scored so high when she had such a horrific upbringing. She replied that because her childhood was of terror and horror, everything she now experienced was always better, and she could celebrate life and living. This is true joy.

Awareness is our basis of joy; awareness is our consciousness and our connection to the Beloved. In being, we become joy as we allow ourselves the beauty of the relationship, the beauty of the creation, and the beauty of our being within such creation. We have been given such gifts in order to remember ourselves as divinity expressed outwardly. Bless such joy, for in joy, we are loved and loving.

In joy, we are also connected to sorrow, for these emotions complement one another. Sorrow is often seen as the opposite of joy, yet sorrow is a feeling that can lead us in our joyfulness. We will continue by focusing on such sorrow.

<u>Chapter Five</u>

THE SACREDNESS OF SORROW

The Guest House

This being human is a guest house.
Every morning a new arrival.
A joy, a depression, a meanness,
some momentary awareness comes
as an unexpected visitor.

Welcome and entertain them all!
Even if they're a crowd of sorrows,
who violently sweep your house
empty of its furniture,
still, treat each guest honorably.
He may be cleaning you out
for some new delight.

The dark thought, the shame, the malice,
meet them at the door laughing,
and invite them in.

Be grateful for whoever comes,
because each has been sent
as a guide from beyond. (1-18)
Rumi (Barks 109)

What is sorrow? Sorrow is a cleansing of our heart, an opening to our soul, a connection to our divinity. Sorrow is about suffering and heartbreak. To allow ourselves to enter sorrow is to give ourselves a most precious life gift — the gift of feeling. Life is about experiencing all levels of feeling, from pain to joy.

We must learn to embrace our sorrows; to cry, scream, sob, wallow; to experience devastation and face death knocking at our door, and to then fill up with life once again. Because sorrow is an emptying process, a death process. Sorrow is also transformative, for it revitalizes the heart and soul. We must allow ourselves to be transformed, from our physical self to our emotional self to our spiritual self. Only by allowing the sorrow to penetrate each level can we allow the healing power we possess to perform its miracle. Without our grief, we would stagnate. With each loss, however, we learn how to soften, to feel deeper levels of compassion, to become stronger, and to learn trust. How trust? Because only when we allow our ego to be totally shattered can we come out on the other side. We learn to allow our faith to carry us over the threshold of despair.

When we grieve, when we feel totally alone, abandoned, and empty, we are never more closely held. The Beloved cries with us, hurts for us, dies a little death along with the breaking of our hearts. But she is there, always lovingly present. Embracing, soothing, transforming, and bathing us in Light, if we only allow ourselves to be open to the experience and to have faith that God is within and without — never apart.

At first, we may merely survive the devastation of our loss. We attempt to put one foot in front of the other, to muddle through our days, days which can feel endless. Time stands still in our sorrow and does so for a reason — so we can learn how to enter our grief and fully embrace it. Through the acceptance of loss, we begin to heal.

We may believe that our suffering may never soften, that we will always feel the grief, the pain, the heartbreak of our loss. And too often, we contribute to our ongoing sorrow by attempting to shut down our feelings, to stifle our heart and deny our soul. Yet the soul remembers each and every loss that is never mourned and the heart begins to disintegrate from our lack of connectedness. Only when we allow the heart to enter into each and every pain, to enter fully into the darkness, can the spirit soar and allow the soul its due.

Grieving is an act of strength. What can be more powerful than fully opening our heart chakra to not only pain, but to healing, joy, and love? Because becoming our authentic selves is truly a courageous act. How much easier it is to wear a mask to hide our true selves, to hide from our feelings, to deny our spirit. To allow ourselves the path of authenticity is an indication that we trust our Source to take us through any experience with grace and dignity, no matter how difficult that experience might be.

Allowing ourselves sorrow is a process of cleansing. A cleansing of the travesties of life by allowing the heart to weep. To weep away all that ails us, to weep away pain and loss, to weep away our shattered existence, to weep and allow the Divine to enter. Tears of joy and tears of sorrow demonstrate different physical properties indicating the very cleansing nature of our grief — to rid ourselves in order to fill ourselves.

As a therapist, I work with people who are experiencing loss and trauma. I have listened to stories of childhood sexual abuse, animal and human sacrifices, gang rapes, crack house murders, head decapitations, deaths of loved ones, suicides, homicides, relationship traumas, and all other types of grief. These individuals who have experienced loss come into therapy to grieve those losses and to hopefully experience a process of healing that allows them to live again, to find their source of strength, and to begin to relate once again to the joys of life.

I worked with one man who had experienced horrible abuse as a child — sexual, physical and emotional abuse — that was perpetrated by his father and uncle. As a young man, he had also perpetrated his young daughter when he was intoxicated, and when this was reported to the Child Protection Agency, he got an attorney. He was able to pass a lie detector test and further legal proceedings were dropped. However, he knew he had sexually abused his daughter and carried the guilt and shame of this into middle adulthood. He eventually sought counseling and began working a 12 step program. He began a path of healing from the traumas of his past and was able to look at his own abusive behavior towards his daughter. This involved incredibly painful work, but he was motivated to do everything he needed to do for himself and for his daughter (now a young adult). In examining his own sorrow, he was able to connect to his daughter's sorrow. He continues to work on his own issues and has begun to focus on his spiritual beliefs.

All types of sorrow, from our personal mourning, to the sorrow we feel for others, to the suffering of the planet, and to archetypal suffering, can take us away from our spiritual core if we allow it. Alienated from divinity, our depression continues to spiral downward if we have nothing to ground us to the Earth and no way to reach the heavens. We may grasp at the threads of what sanity is left, but without our connection to the Source, our grasp remains tenuous.

But over time, if we are open to the All, we begin to transcend survival and move into a mode of thriving, to again feel a connection with life. To find pleasure in day-to-day activities; to experience joy, compassion, friendship, love. To embrace the beauty of existence and to then, once again, dive into the depths of sorrow. With each and every loss, with each new heartbreak, we become stronger. We begin to see the interconnectedness of life and our role in it. And while we embrace this interaction with life, we also learn how to detach and detach with love. We recognize that no matter what happens to us, we are divine love and divinely loved. No experience, no matter how horrendous, how heart wrenching, can destroy us or keep us from our core, which is love.

To allow our grief its process, we need to create a sanctuary. A safe, loving space in which to allow ourselves to wail, to empty, to fill. This space needs to be both internal and external. Internal space of allowing our hearts to feel the painful experiences; external, private spaces where we can safely lose ourselves in the process. An altar in a room, a secret nest in the woods, a hidden place by the water — anywhere that is a sanctuary which we can claim as our own is valuable in cleansing our inner and outer houses.

I wrap my sorrow around me like a blanket

to cocoon me in its safety of pain.

A sanctuary of grief that allows me to

break open my abandoned heart.

Shattering my psyche.

Destroying my fragile hold on reality

with a terrifying tenacity.

Pain that I have experienced for many lifetimes.

Annihilating the existence that I've formerly known.

Picking up the shattered fragments of my heart,

and stitching them together

in a kaleidoscope of healing.

DEPRESSION, GRIEF, SPIRITUAL SORROW

We can classify our sadness into three types: depression, grief, and spiritual sorrow. And while we examine these three types of sorrow, we must remember that all of them exist for a purpose. The demons in our lives are meant to be experienced, exorcised, and exonerated. Losing our sanity in order to find our sanity is the process of sorrow.

DEPRESSION

Disappointment, disillusionment, depression, despair, darkness — a continuum of struggles defined by sorrow. Often these states are categorized as states of depression, although depression is a misnomer for four of these conditions. These life issues may lead to an actual state of depression, but they are not necessarily depressive conditions, per se.

Disappointment is about unrealized hopes, dreams, and expectations. Disappointment is a feeling state related to somehow "missing the mark." All of us have experienced disappointment in our lives, from not getting a job promotion, to losing in a sporting event, to not receiving the hoped for phone call from a potential suitor. Most of us overcome our disappointment with a modicum of psychic effort.

Disillusionment is related to being unable to free ourselves from our illusions, whether these illusions are related to false ideas about ourselves, others, or the world itself. Dissatisfaction and discontentment are components of disillusionment, the feeling of lack of gratification with life situations, sometimes a sense of malaise. Disillusionment may require more of our emotional, psychological, and spiritual energy in order to grow, but again, all of us experience disillusionment in life and most of us walk through it without too much difficulty.

But when we are truly talking about clinical depression, we are usually referring to one of two types: dysthymia or major depression. Dysthymia is a low-lying depression that lasts for years and often begins in childhood. It may or may not interfere with our daily tasks, yet it is pervasive and causes us to feel as though we aren't functioning at full capacity. The sense is one of "the blues." Dysthymia has some of the same symptoms as major depression, just at a lesser intensity.

Major depression is characterized by a lack of emotion or endless sadness and weeping, a lack of connection to life, an emptiness without hope. There is a void of energy, the experience of anhedonia (the inability to feel pleasure) and dysphoria (irritability, restlessness, malaise). Feelings of sadness, inadequacy, guilt and shame may be overpowering. We begin to withdraw and isolate. Concentration and memory problems become pervasive as does the inability to have many conscious thoughts. Sleep, appetite, and sexual interests usually decrease although sleep may increase as a way to check out of life. Exhaustion begins to set in as the entire physiological system continues to shut down. There is seldom any future orientation; how can one focus on the future when death is being experienced presently? Preoccupation with death and suicide may develop and suicide attempts may be made.

Depression may be a physiological/biological (including genetic) condition, it may be learned (growing up with someone who is depressed can teach us to respond to life with a depressed outlook), or it may be situational (the loss of a job, a child moving out of the home) or it may be a combination of causes. Grief that isn't processed may result in depression. Grief is a natural healing process; depression is not. Depression is an illness.

Sucked into the abyss of my soul,

a shadow around my deadened heart.

A skeletal tomb of feeling,

of thought,

of existence.

"You can't be depressed, you're too funny."

"You aren't the person I used to know."

"What's wrong with you?"

And a personal favorite, "Pull yourself up

by your bootstraps."

"What bootstraps? I don't even have a boot."

Boot: an instrument of torture for crushing

: to kick, as to punish

: to dismiss

: to error, screw up, fail.

Depression, despair, darkness.

Sinking, sick, suffering, suffocating.

iwannadieiwannadieiwannadieiwannadieiwannadie

A Gregorian chant.

I remember working with a woman a number of years ago who came to see me because she was experiencing poor sleep, poor appetite, overwhelming feelings of malaise, visual hallucinations, self-harm behaviors (cutting and burning), and thoughts of death and suicide. She had horrible cuts on her thighs and arms that left huge scars. I felt she needed to be placed on antidepressant and antipsychotic medications and she did follow through with this. We began to explore her history of depression as well as her alcoholism, drug addictions, and self–mutilation, which were used to cover up her pain of a childhood that offered little emotional support, sexual abuse by an older cousin, and a mother too impaired by her own depression to provide any support. With the combination of medication and therapy she began to heal, but it was a process of four years. Yet she began to feel that something was missing and this was her connection to the Universe. This individual began to pray and meditate and became involved with a church community. She also refocused on her connection to nature. She read books on recovery for her addictions and books exploring spiritually. She allowed herself to go to the depths of her pain and heal from this. She is one of the success stories.

But there are so many stories of people who do not get well and continue to suffer throughout their lifetimes. Overwhelming thoughts of death and dying, sometimes accompanied by visual and auditory hallucinations. Suicide attempts that failed; medications that didn't work.

Depression is often quickly treated with medication or if the condition is more severe and doesn't respond to medication, electroconvulsive therapy (ECT) may be utilized. And hopefully the person being treated is also utilizing the benefits of psychotherapy, a process of examining one's emotional, cognitive, and behavioral responses to life. Yet while these treatments are successful, they must not be the sole (soul) treatment. Because medication does not heal the soul, ECT does not shock us out of our spiritual malaise, and traditional therapy typically ignores the value of melancholy.

Inherent in depression is a propensity towards growth. Depression is the indication that something is out of balance in our lives and that this something needs our attention. Psychologist John Welwood indicates that:

> Depression sets in when we conclude that there is something basically wrong with us because we experience pain, we feel vulnerable or sad, we cannot hold on to our achievements, or we discover the hollowness of our self-created identity. In feeling this hollowness of identity, we are very close to experiencing the larger openness of our being. (162)

This "larger openness of our being" must be addressed. No medication, no medical treatment can heal this aspect of our self. We must allow ourselves to experience transformation at a deeper level.

This type of depression may not be clinical depression, but that of melancholy. Thomas Moore in *Care of the Soul* tells us that, "Melancholy gives the soul an opportunity to express a side of its nature that is as valid as any other, but is hidden out of our distaste for its darkness and bitterness" (138). We need to look at the positive intention of melancholy because by its very nature, it is providing an opportunity for growth. Perhaps it is to teach us that it is time to change our responses to life's ups and downs; perhaps to teach us that in order to experience joy, we must experience the darkness; perhaps to teach us that living includes pain and grief and that death is a process of living in this human existence. All of our experiences must be embraced in order to fully understand the needs of Spirit. Our very existence is about the lightness and darkness of humanity and of the cosmos — embracing both is embracing the dialectic of divinity.

Pain, as we have already seen, can cleanse our inner house, and can open the window to healing and intimacy with ourselves, others, and Goddess. This window of opportunity opens us to the darkness that lurks within so we can embrace the loneliness, despair, and emptiness, and know that it is of Mother Earth and Father Sky, and that it is there to help guide us.

Despair and darkness are deeper levels of the psyche which take us beyond the level of what we usually think of as depression. Despair and darkness will be addressed in the section "Spiritual Sorrow." Let us now move into an exploration of grief.

GRIEF

Your pain is the breaking of the shell

that encloses your understanding.

Even as the stone of the fruit must break,

that its heart may stand in the sun, so must

you know pain.

And could you keep your heart in wonder

at the daily miracles of your life, your pain

would not seem less wondrous than your

joy;

And you would accept the seasons of your

heart, even as you have always accepted

the seasons that pass over your fields.

And you would watch with serenity

through the winters of your grief. (4-17)

                                        Gibran (52)

    Grief is our natural healing response to loss — the loss of childhood
innocence through abuse, the death of a loved one, a divorce, an illness,
children leaving home. Life is about loss, grief is the emotion related to the
loss, and mourning is the processing of the loss, although grieving and
mourning are often used synonymously.
    Grief is often misidentified as depression although unresolved grief
often turns into depression. Why misidentified? Perhaps because we are so
frightened of our grief, fearful of the pain, often gut-wrenching pain that
may accompany the loss. How terrifying it is to allow our hearts to be
ripped apart. How much easier it is to try to pass grief off as depression so
that we can pop a pill and hope that it disappears. But pills don't treat grief;
only by walking through the garden of our sorrow can we heal.
    Mourning is not something that waits for us to be ready in order to expe-
rience it. Grief is there in our face, demanding our attention. It has its own
time frame and its own agenda. Grief may visit us in the form of shock, numbness, denial, and disbelief, or in the form of tumultuous feelings such as rage,
anxiety, fear, and overwhelming sadness. It may show itself in bargaining
("Please God, if you heal me from this illness, I'll . . ."), through withdrawal
from life, or with an overwhelming burst of activity. This sorrow may present
itself in the form of physical or emotional illness. We may find ourselves wailing or wallowing in our pain. Our dreams may become more vivid and they
may constantly replay the nature of our loss and disrupt our sleep.
    Yet if we allow our grief to flow through us, we begin to move beyond.
We understand that sorrow is as much a part of creation as is joy. We must
allow suffering to be suffering. And then, we go on. We can choose to live and
embrace what life offers us both in birth and in death. In our choice, the
Divine is always present.
    As we wind our way through our grief, we begin to integrate the loss
into the context of our lives. We may move into a period of solitude or we
may begin to enjoy the connection we have with other persons. We begin
to relate to life itself. We reorganize our lives. We pick up the pieces and

carry on. We begin to have hopes and dreams; we experience pleasure and on occasion begin to feel joy. We connect with life as life is.

Watching people heal through the transformation of grief is an incredible experience. I have watched thousands of people in therapy do amazing things through the strength of their spirits. I have also watched many people struggle to embrace this process; individuals who have remained stuck in their sorrow. Yet even such "stuckness" is a process on the path to change and enlightenment, for in our ruts, we can learn how to climb out of the darkness — or not.

Joe was a Vietnam veteran who suffered from post-traumatic stress disorder (PTSD) and alcoholism. I saw him for therapy for three years. His PTSD resulted in a psychic numbing of his pain, numbing that was also increased by his drinking. He suffered from horrific flashbacks and nightmares. His increased startle reaction was evidenced when the Blue Angels fighter planes flew overhead in a local festival; Joe thought he was back in Vietnam and would "hit the deck" in response to the noise. He was able to tell me about his symptoms, but he refused to tell me about his experiences in Vietnam stating, "Carol, I like you too much to tell you the atrocities I saw and committed there." No matter how much I encouraged him to talk and told him that I'd heard many horrific stories in my lifetime, he could not share them — as much for his own psychic wellbeing as for my own. These traumas continued to haunt him into his 50s when he died from cirrhosis of the liver as a result of his drinking. Joe died a tortured man — unable to reconcile his terror and grief. And while he was able to do some grieving in therapy, he could not get beyond his own pain. Perhaps in the next lifetime. . . .

Yet out of grief is birthed a new reality. A realization that we can go on, that we now have an even greater capacity for love and compassion, and that we can survive anything and are stronger for it. We also learn that we are connected to Gaia and to the cosmos for we are never separate. We understand that if we let go and trust the Beloved with our process of grief, eventually our roses will again bloom and bless us in their beauty and fragrance. We recognize the meaning of grace and we live within that grace — blessing and being blessed.

I am learning the lessons of aloneness.

Of letting go of everything and everyone

that I thought defined me -

Including you.

Detachment.

Silence.

I walk alone. . .

but do I?

Never alone — always closely held.

The Beloved.

SPIRITUAL SORROW

The third type of sorrow is that of spiritual sorrow. Spiritual sorrow is sometimes seen as an existential grief, existentialism being a philosophy that focuses on the meaning of life. Existentialism examines our longing for meaning, our desire for relief from alienation, our search for understanding in our day-to-day existence, an understanding of our despair and anguish. Questions related to our existential crisis include: Who am I? What is the meaning of life? Why do I suffer? Is this all there is? Why do I exist? Where can peace of mind or happiness be found? This despair one experiences in searching for one's self may lead to a new level of faith and an exploration of the spiritual self. While spiritual sorrow is an entity in and of itself, it may be triggered by other mood states such as depression or grief, thus exacerbating the pain.

Spiritual sorrow is the deepest level of sorrow we can manifest on this human level, although it is beyond human. It is the sorrow of our soul, a longing for a connection of our humanity with our divinity. It is felt at a depth of which has been previously unknown. There is a sense of emptiness, a void, a nothingness, an abyss of blinding darkness. This goes beyond a feeling of spiritual malaise into a pain that permeates each and every level of the psyche — a soul-wrenching anguish that cannot be overcome. We may feel overwhelmingly despondent, as though we are in such a pit of despair that we might never climb out. We may feel as though we are being tortured from within and without, yet the torturing event cannot be identified (because there is none). We may find ourselves wailing without end, pleading to God to end this hell. This sorrow may feel like death and, in fact, we are dying on some level. Dying to an old way of life, a dying of our false ego which often struggles to maintain itself with a stubborn tenacity, a dying of our humanity into a higher level of being.

This despair may be experienced as the surreal, a feeling of an altered state of existence, an experience of depersonalization and dissociation.

This sense of unreality may be quite disconcerting as there is no sense of being grounded to anything familiar in life. We may feel that we are walking into another realm of existence, a realm beyond the usual time/space continuum. Floating into another dimension on a cloud of surreal-ness.

Other states may also be experienced during the intensity of this sorrow: visions, hallucinations, anxiety, fear, terror, nightmares, vivid dreams, death images, suicidal thoughts, and out-of-body experiences. All of our previous realities may become distorted; our thoughts, beliefs, and values will be challenged. Nothing may be familiar. Things that were once meaningful are now meaningless. Things that were once purposeful are now purposeless. Things that were once valuable are now valueless.

Within this crisis of spirit, there is no connection with life of any sort, including nature, family and friends, and more soul-wrenching, no connection to All That Is. Christina and Stanislav Grof relate, "During the existential crisis, one feels cut off from the deeper self, higher power, or God — whatever one depends on beyond personal resources to provide strength and inspiration. The result is a most devastating kind of loneliness, a total and complete existential alienation that penetrates one's entire being" (53). The barrenness of this crisis is pervasive.

These experiences indicate that we are in a period of spiritual emergency, which has also been described as the Dark Night of the Soul. We return to Grof and Grof who describe the difference between spiritual emergence and spiritual emergency. Spiritual emergence is the "movement of an individual to a more expanded way of being that involves enhanced emotional and psychosomatic health, greater freedom of personal choices, and a sense of deeper connection with other people, nature and the cosmos" (34). A spiritual emergency, however, is a difficult and painful stage in which there is a "profound psychological transformation that involves one's entire being" (31) and involves the aforementioned states of reality in which the system of the individual feels disorganized, disoriented, and chaotic. This is also the experience of the dark night.

I watched a friend of mine go through such a spiritual emergency — an emergency that neither one of us understood. This friend is a bright, creative individual who has traveled the world, speaks three languages, and works in upper management at a Fortune 500 company. She had never been in therapy prior to this spiritual emergency; she had no history of mental illness, horrific childhood trauma or addiction, and there was no history of mental illness in the family. But she began experiencing terrifying nightmares, flashbacks, and daymares of murders in which she participated. She felt as though she was actually in these visions because they seemed so real. For the first time in her life, she became fearful of herself and her own capacity for evil. She also had detailed fantasies of killing people currently in her life; of stabbing them to death and enjoying such horror. We explored her history and I asked her if she needed medical attention; perhaps these visions were being caused by a tumor or other medical crisis. We discussed if she needed psychiatric medication, but she felt this was something she needed to work through. She did not feel she was in the throes of a mental illness.

During this time period, she sought counseling and she eventually found a counselor that was able to walk her through this trauma. They were able to identify this as a spiritual emergency, a dark night of the soul, and that her visions were from past lifetimes. They were able to process these lifetimes and my friend began to heal from the past trauma. Had she not found such an excellent counselor, she probably would have eventually been treated in the mental health system and placed on antipsychotic medication, and the whole process of working through this spiritual emergency would never have taken place. Through this experience she has become stronger and has found a much deeper connection to her spirit and the soul of the universe; her individual soul knew what she needed.

The Dark Night of the Soul is a process often described, but seldom understood. Frequently, this process has come to mean any hardship that is experienced in life. But not all difficulties, sorrows, traumas, or losses are true dark nights; they are more simply life traumas. Perhaps we need to return to the origin of the dark night and explore what St. John of the Cross distinguishes as the night of the sense versus the night of the spirit. Because often what is described as the dark night of the soul (which is the night of the spirit) is in actuality, the night of the sense or the first night of sensual purgation, which is commonly experienced (32-33).

This first night is of the senses and is where the body purges the emotions, while the other night is that of spiritual purgation where the soul is "purified and detached in the spirit, and which subdues and disposes it for union with God in love. The night of the sense is common, and the lot of many: these are the beginners [. . .]. The spiritual night is the portion of very few [. . .]" (32). Both of these nights are painful and difficult.

We all go through the purging of the emotions and the physical senses in our journey towards our Higher Power for this is the beginning of the healing of our sorrow. All traumas and losses are related to the purging of our senses; this is what grieving is about. And we must go through the trauma of the senses in order to progress into the purgation of the higher self.

Others of us will continue into the Night of the Spirit which is the "pain and torment" of the soul, what is usually written about as the Dark Night. In the dark night, the pain of the soul includes: 1) the darkness of the self that is revealed in the light of God; 2) the weakness of the self that is felt under God's strength; 3) the loss of God which is felt in the sense of unworthiness; 4) an emptiness of self which is felt through the fullness of God; 5) remembering past happiness and being unable to experience it; and

6) the inability to focus upon God and divinity (St. John 75-92). These traumas lead to letting go of our intellect, our will, and our ego in order to merge into union with the Beloved in illumination and enlightenment.

In the Dark Night, the sorrow becomes torturous in the emptying of the heart and soul. The darkness of the abyss, the annihilation of the spirit, the pain and suffering, the emptiness and abandonment, and the pure desolation, eventually give way to a burst of light and love. Because without the crucifixion there is no resurrection.

The surreal-ness of a Salvador Dali painting,

time melting off the table,

while standing still in my existence of grief.

Unreality, floating in a warp of time and space.

Surreal-ness shifts to the terror of Hieronymus Bosch,

horrifying trauma, torture, excruciating pain, fear, death,

- painted in exquisite detail

- exposing the hunted and the haunted.

Eventually lifting to the desolateness of Andrew Wyeth.

When will I ever enter a Monet?

The dark night, with its two levels of process, must be honored in its entirety. We must examine both and not trivialize the "lesser" night of the sense. We need to explore these small dark nights and the gifts they are offering because they are gifts. The small dark nights sometimes begin in childhood where our ego identity has yet to be fully established, yet the spirit recognizes that it is a process of sorrow. With each and every night of the sense, layer upon layer of the human psyche is peeled away — peeled away in order to reach our core of divinity. We may eventually reach the night of the spirit through these mini-deaths — or not. The importance is to honor the divinity in each and every sorrow we experience.

Like many of us, my friend in the story above had gone through instances of the night of the sense, where she had grief to work through with losses such as a breakup with a significant other and the deaths of loved ones. She was, on her own, able to work through these losses by grieving them and going on with her life. But her true Dark Night was the loss of her connection with herself and with Goddess. She was almost paralyzed by the overwhelming torment that she experienced. Yet this torment was there to help her to grow into her highest self, for out of abandonment comes connection.

In counseling I work with people who are going through the night of the sense. This is the process of therapy — to purge and to heal the senses — as trauma and losses are to be felt, healed, and let go into transformation of the self. Yet I have also worked with a few people who went beyond these losses and who were experiencing the night of the spirit. These individuals felt these losses to the level of the soul and felt disconnected from themselves and from the Divine. This terrible darkness encompassed their beings as they felt a void of existence, an emptiness of self, and a disconnection from the Oneness. With much work and faith, they were able to work through these dark nights of the soul.

These are the incredible journeys that we go through as human beings, and I am grateful not only for my own journey, but also for the thousands of people who have shared their journeys with me in faith, trust, and companionship. For as one person heals, we all heal.

Our spiritual sorrow, from the night of the sense to the night of the spirit, is our longing for union with the Absolute. There is no greater pain than that of separation from the Sacred. We long with every aspect of our being to be connected, to merge fully into Oneness. We search and search to find meaning in our everyday existence only to be thwarted in our connection. But there is meaning in this. This emptiness of our being is there for us to enter into the longing, the desire, and the reverence of the connection. Because through faith, the connection will come. With patience, with endurance, through pain and trauma, through a void in our heart and soul, the connection will come.

In our spiritual sorrow we come to understand and embrace the value of chaos, for chaos is of the spirit, the soul, and the universe. Chaos theory in physics reveals that what appears to be chaotic in the universe has an underlying basis of order. We must allow chaos to be chaos; it is there for a purpose — to vitalize the energy flowing around and through us. Chaos, whether it be of depression, of grief, or of a dark night, provides an opportunity for the system to cleanse, to work through, and reorganize and revitalize the internal state of the individual. Healthy chaos allows us to transform, but we must be careful not to allow the chaos to become dysfunctional and keep us trapped in an endless spinning of spiritual emergency.

This healthy chaos is a process of our sorrow. We don't just experience one dark night of the soul; we experience it over and over again. Why? Because each sorrow, each night of the sense that we successfully maneuver, leads us to growth and healing beyond the crisis and the chaos into a higher level of understanding in order to reach our destination which is to become one with the Source. To empty ourselves in order to fill ourselves with the glory of the Beloved is the outcome of such sorrow.

So do we dive into the sorrow of our existence and trust that a regeneration of life will develop, or do we stay in a fear-based mentality of maintaining the status quo, or worse, sink further into the limitations of our human self? We must let go of the halfhearted functioning and melt into the fire of our spirit in order to set it free. To set free is to let go of our expectations, our life plans, our worries and willfulness, our manipulations of others, our addictive behaviors, our denials, and our doing-ness. In the end, it is the letting go of the ego and doing "Thy will." Doing "Thy will" by trusting, always trusting, that the Great Spirit will carry us through all the trials and tribulations of this human existence. And by letting go of the false ego, the trials and tribulations no longer exist as we now understand that there is a divine purpose and a divine plan in our lives and that we openly embrace them all. The mystery is a part of the plan. Union with the Beloved is the purpose.

Stripped to the core,
I stand naked before you.

Chapter Six

SHADOW AND BEYOND SHADOW

We see so much evil around us,
so much harm done,
that we think it impossible
that there is any good in this world.

We look at this in sorrow
and mourn so
that we cannot see God as we should.

This is because we use our reason
so blindly, so unfully
and so simplemindedly
that we are unable to know
the marvelous wisdom, capability
and goodness
of the joyful Trinity. (1-14)

Julian of Norwich (Doyle 56)

While we all have our shadow selves — those repressed unconscious parts of our ego — there are some persons who go beyond the shadow into the level of evil. What is the difference? The shadow is our disowned humanity, the parts of ourselves that cause us (and others) dissonance. The shadow lurks around our very being, hidden in the subconscious, but asking to be acknowledged and wanting to be brought forth into light in order to be fully healed. Evil, in contrast, can permeate our entire being without ever wanting to come into the light. In fact, it tries to bring others into the darkness. Yes, it wants to be acknowledged, but acknowledged not to transform into healing, but for its power, its complete darkness, its insidiousness, its emptiness of the soul.

Shadow is of the ego, of the human personality, and can be healed when it is openly recognized and conscious work is done towards transformation. Evil too, can be healed, but it is a much more difficult process because it does not want healing and because it is a much deeper level of darkness, often to the level of the soul. Shadow and evil are enacted on a continuum of possibilities. Yet it is difficult to understand where the shadow begins to turn into evil. And underlying both shadow and evil is goodness, for we are born into the Light. Both the human personality and the soul essence may develop into evil, but the basis of humanity is goodness.

In attempting to explore the dynamics of good and evil, we must let go of the notion that it is a dichotomy; instead, it must be examined as a dialectic, a both/and relationship. Without goodness there would be no evil; without evil, there would be no goodness. For in our creation, the Creator birthed all that could exist, and in order to have one type of experience, the opposite experience must also exist. The essence of goodness and the essence of darkness come from the source of divine being. Let us explore the depths of ourselves.

I'm tired of running from myself — so

I don't anymore.

But those I love keep running.

Running, running, running,

like lemmings to the sea.

Escape in a drowning of fear.

That from which I try to escape

escapes me.

Lemmings with Nikes.

SHADOW

What is shadow? We turn to humanist psychologist Carl Jung who states: "By shadow I mean the 'negative' side of the personality, the sum of all those unpleasant qualities we like to hide, together with the insufficiently developed functions and the contents of the personal unconscious" (Storr 87). The shadow is that part of us that relates to our morality and our spirituality, for only in exploring the dark places within the unconscious can we truly grow. The shadow is a moral dilemma, the negative qualities of a personality that violate one's value system. It is a conflict of the ego — does the ego really want to acknowledge that there is a darker side to its personality? It is a painful process to first admit and then accept that darkness resides within. This negativity must eventually come to consciousness in order for the system to heal and grow beyond its limitations.

Jung relates that the shadow, being the repressed piece of the personality, is "merely somewhat inferior, primitive, unadapted, and awkward; not wholly bad" (Storr 90). The characteristics of shadow are those qualities that don't fit our personal definition of self, that go against our stated value system, that are the dark spots in what we believe is our healthy personality. Think of those aspects of others that you really dislike: being judgmental, rude, envious, selfish, cruel, etc. Can you identify these same traits in yourself? How easy it is to identify others' character flaws, but how difficult it is to recognize the shadow side of ourselves. This is called projection, a part of the ego which attributes what we don't like about ourselves onto someone else in an effort to keep the darkness in the unconscious through denial. Yet others clearly see our shadow; it is repressed only to ourselves.

So how do we come to terms with our own shadow, or do we? Some of the options are to run and hide from it; deny it exists; do nothing about it; project it upon others, i.e., instead of "I'm so angry," I state, "I can't believe how angry she is"; or to acknowledge it and work toward bringing it to the light.

In reality, most of us have tried the first practices without success. We've tried denial, projection, control and irresponsibility, only to have the shadow knock on the door of our consciousness and tell us that these fee-ble attempts are not working. When the pain and suffering of the ego gets so overwhelming, then and only then will we attempt the process of accept-ing the darkness and transforming all of its creative energy into growth of the personality.

In our shadow work, ego meets Divine, and we must begin to allow the true nature of the self to shine forth. We need to listen to the heart and soul of the inner voice in order to understand, experience, and accept the darkness within, because the shadow can offer us so much on our journey into creation. The shadow has its own values and its own meanings that allow it to help the ego to transform. But when we begin our shadow work, only a strong, healthy ego can undergo the intense scrutiny that takes place with this inner work, an ego that can accept that there is darkness within the human personality and that embraces such darkness as a way to transform. This is the ego born of openness, trust, and connection to the inner divinity we all experience. This is the ego born of love and compassion. It is the wisdom of the Beloved and based in the grace, the flexibility, and the strength of our true selves. For the shadow does not go away; it merely transforms from the darkness into the light. It has its own wisdom that offers growth.

How so wisdom? Because everything about ourselves speaks its own truth and the shadow has much to teach us. It has its own energy, its own life force that vitalizes our very souls. Remember that without darkness we could not perceive the lightness and that this dialectical relationship is also a symbiotic one — they need each other to expand. Until we examine our shadows, we remain stuck in an existence of denial and half truths, never fully trusting the Source in guiding us through all our experiences. Only through the darkness can we transform our human ego self into the divine self.

What stops us from moving into evil is the chore of bringing our shadow to the conscious from the unconscious. We all have disowned, dis-liked aspects of the self that cause us to fear our own capabilities. But by acknowledging and embracing the shadow, these parts of ourselves no longer fester in our depths waiting to burst forth with intense, and some-times harmful expressions. As psychiatrist M. Scott Peck tells us:

> . . . it is necessary that we first draw the distinction between evil and ordinary sin. It is not their sins per se that characterize evil people, rather it is the subtlety and persistence and consistency of their sins. This is because the central defect of the evil is not the sin but the refusal to acknowledge it. (69)

So it is not the sin or shadow that is evil, since we have all done things that go against our own values. Rather it is the denial, the dissociation, the lies, and the cover-ups that lead to evil acts and evil beings.

The friend that I discussed earlier about going though grief and a dark night was facing her shadow. In her violent dreams and violent thoughts, she was able to work with her counselor to face her demons. For in facing her demons, she was able to bring her shadow into the light, therefore pre-empting the possibly of doing evil by acting upon such horrific thoughts.

Within our shadow there may be extreme talent. Creativity is not only of goodness, but also of darkness, and we must listen to these dark forces as they have much to tell us. They relate that life is painful with its trauma and despair, sorrow and loss, hate and damnation, fear and faithlessness. The dark creative forces speak to us and tell us when it is time to move on, to change our focus or to die a death on physical, emotional, or spiritual planes of existence. The darkness can lead into lightness through creative expression. If we paint, talk, feel, sing, meditate, pray, dance, or write through the shadow, we heal at a deeper level of existence for these are the practices that expand the soul.

I once worked with a middle-aged man who told me he sexually abused a girl at a camp where he was a camp counselor many years ago. He could not remember her name, but discussed details about how he perpe-trated her, using his good looks and charismatic nature to entice her to his bed (she was 13, he was 21). He had never told anyone and felt tremen-dous shame about it. He adamantly stated he had never done this again, but he still had thoughts of sexually abusing young women. Once he talked about his darkness, he was able to let go of some of his shame. This was a very creative man and we used his artistic talent of painting and his joy of playing the piano to help him heal from his darkness and capacity to do evil acts. He used art to allow himself to feel his own feelings of being sexu-ally abused when he was a child and rid himself of the shame of his sexual abuse and that of the girl he abused. He was able to be open and honest about the abuse and his responsibility of not harming anyone again. The last time I had contact with him, he was doing well in his recovery.

Yet darkness is creative in its own right. Think of some of your favorite books or movies that relate to horror and fear. Are these not works created by talented individuals who have tapped into their own shadows as well as the shadows of their audiences? Being able to honor our own dark creative forces is just another means of expression and if this creativity is expressed in such a positive way, it stops the shadow from building to extreme levels which could lead to destructively creative expression.

I am always reading two types of books — spirituality texts and mystery novels. The mysteries that are my favorite are ones that make me think — where I am able to form my own hypothesis about the murder. Is this my darker self? I believe so, yet it is also a creative side of me. In another life I must have been some type of detective or profiler as it is a way for me to put together pieces of a puzzle, similar to the puzzle pieces I put together in working with therapy clients. It taps into my rather methodical, obsessive nature as well as my therapist role of exploring human nature. So while it might be an aspect of my shadow side, it doesn't turn into evil as I acknowledge it and bring it into the light energy of life. Now if I started acting out such murders, then we would have to begin exploring my slide into evil.

Within the shadow may be the fear of extreme talent. We are all destined to greatness, to be our fullest divine selves, and this is often a terrifying reality. It is so much easier to live a life of denial, limitation, and complacency than to explore the essence of being a creative, multi-talented child of God. For if I must admit that I have such talents, then I might have to put them into action, thereby disrupting the status quo and making major life changes. If this creativity stays hidden in the denial of the shadow, I do not have to be responsible for what I am called upon to do.

Therapy is a creative process which allows one to do his or her shadow work. Many people, including myself, have gone into therapy in order to try to fix, control, or manipulate others or the environment around them. While this may be the initial goal of clients, it becomes apparent this is not possible, and they begin to work on exploring their issues and changing their thoughts, feelings, and behaviors. In this work, individuals now begin to explore their own shadows and how to bring their shadows into consciousness in order to change and adapt to others and the world around them.

For example, I remember years ago of going into therapy to try to "fix" my partner because she wasn't behaving the way I wanted. I was certain she was having an affair and I was finding her behaviors to be manipulative and dishonest. I would catch her in lies which she would adamantly deny; for example, listening to her lie to our paperboy about paying him when she hadn't; someone calling me about how she was avoiding his calls as she owned him money for an event he conducted; stealing from her work and justifying her behavior. She also began to do little mind games, such as sneaking into our apartment and moving a trash can or paper just enough for me to know she had been there, but not returning home at night. She began to feel creepy but I was unwilling to see the truth as I remained in denial. I felt that somehow I could make her better and make her into the person I wanted her to be. But I soon realized that the inner work that had to be done was my own. I needed to look at my own shadow qualities that were attracted to her darkness. I realized I was attracted to her intelligence, her seductiveness, and her unhealthy chaotic behaviors. When she threatened to harm me physically, I immediately moved out of our home. And I eventually realized this was a person who was not only operating from her shadow, but her behavior was sliding into evil.

In working with our individual shadow, we help the collective universe in freeing it from being involved in our moral dilemma. Because if we all do our individual work, the universe embraces the lightness as a collective spirit thus helping it to remain free of a larger darkness. We all have the capacity for good and for evil and the capacity for both increases as we fully come into our power as creative spiritual beings.

EVIL

As already noted, evil forms when we neglect our inner work and don't address the shadow. The shadow itself is not evil, but if left alone to steep in denial and limitation, it can begin to slip into evil. Shadow and evil are on a continuum — how easy it is to become corrupted by the darkness. How effortlessly we can be seduced by its creative insidiousness. For we have been given free will, and in our free will, we can choose whether to go toward the light or towards the dark, thus creating our own goodness or our own evil. For, "The deliberate decision to *do* evil leads to our becoming evil. This is why living out the darkest impulses of the Shadow cannot be a solution to the shadow problem, for we can easily become possessed by or absorbed into evil if we try such a thing" (Sanford 30).

Free will allows the human personality (ego) to be corrupted by evil and a weak ego may choose evil as an attempt to glorify itself through the power of destruction. Yet the soul can also become evil. Even though souls do not begin as evil, they can become so disconnected from the goodness of the Divine that evil can enter. Or a soul may choose to connect with a human body that is very immature in its own right and that will allow the darkness to be the force of the ego. A soul that is struggling in its own development may not be able to impact an evil personality or it may even combine its own life-draining energy (evil) to that of the life-draining personality. We learn that, "The personality sometimes appears as a force running rampant in the world with no attachment to the energy of its soul. This situation can be the origin of what we call an evil human being [. . .]" (Zukav 37). Thus, our human personality, the soul, and free will are all forces that act upon our turning towards goodness or towards evil.

While many of us have experienced evil at some point in life, the nature of evil is so smooth, so slippery, so insidious, and is so thoroughly disguised, the person who has experienced it may be unable to define the experience. And that is evil itself — so difficult to capture. Evil is a chameleon that camouflages itself in many different colors, shapes, and sizes and it loves to change in order to confuse. It plays an "uncanny game of hide-and-seek in the obscurity of the soul, in which it, the single human soul, evades itself, avoids itself, hides from itself" (Buber 111). It also evades, avoids, and hides from others in this same game of hide-and-seek.

M. Scott Peck's classic text, *People of the Lie*, offers a thorough analysis of evil. Although evil is slippery, deceptive and insidious, Peck describes some of its common characteristics. Deception can be unmasked if one knows what to examine. These characteristics of an evil being include: self deception, creating confusion, deceit, scapegoating through projection of their own evil onto others, the complete level of narcissism and lack of empathy for others, refusal to admit to their own shadow, fear of exposure, the mask of "goodness" that they wear, and the sensitivity and fragility of their own outward appearances and respectability.

In the presence of evil, one who is not evil may experience the sensation of revulsion. Peck states, "Evil is revolting because it is dangerous. It will contaminate or otherwise destroy a person who remains too long in its presence" (65). A therapist friend in talking about a mutual acquaintance, whom we both felt was evil, stated that if this person had come to her for therapy, she would have been in her roller chair moving as far away as she could from this individual — this is the experience of revulsion.

Other characteristics would include a pseudo-spirituality, being charismatic, intelligent and creative, and having a relationship to the underworld. While not all evil persons have these traits, persons who do are ones who may become even more entrapped by their own insidiousness, as they are capable of going to greater lengths of destruction.

Evil persons often are disguised through a pseudo-spirituality, an intellectual (and only intellectual) knowledge of religious and spiritual principles used to prove their connection with goodness and godliness. They often hide in religious institutions and may moralize about evil and how to eradicate it. They attempt to show that they are above reproach through the involvement with church or other spiritual activities. They may be present in fundamentalist churches or in New Age practices — no religious institution or practice is exempt. The evil may attempt to use the power of the church not only to justify their own means, but in an attempt to corrupt others who are searching for something on their spiritual path, as well as attempting to corrupt the entire religious institution.

One such woman was an active participant in her church, serving on committees and also was on the Board of Directors. She spoke of her life in spiritual terms, wore her gold cross daily, and presented with religious piety. However, I knew she'd had affairs with two married men in the congregation (she was single) and she talked about how she would sit in the front of the church to try to "seduce" the male minister (also married). She had already devastated two families with her behavior and she was attempting to corrupt another person. For while these men were responsible for their own behavior, her dark seduction was a call that few men refused. What made this evil behavior versus shadow behavior? It was the glee that she experienced after her conquests and it was the refusal to admit her behavior was inappropriate ("They wanted it, so how am I at fault?"). It was the intent of the destructiveness, all under the guise of spirituality.

Charismatic persons who are evil are also dangerous. Because charismatic individuals tend to become leaders who can convert the masses, this type of evil can lead to destruction on a larger basis. We need only look at the likes of Hitler, Jim Jones, bin Laden, and Saddam Hussein to see the power of evil in its ability to corrupt. They also have the ability to corrupt not only those other persons who may be evil, but those persons who have weak souls and egos and who may need to feel a sense of belonging to a person, a group, or a cause (think about youth gangs). Those individuals who may be unaware that evil exists may become indoctrinated into the deceit before they can fully understand what has happened. This is the power of charisma utilized to demonstrate control and to destroy.

Innate intelligence and creativity are other characteristics that can fan a deeper level of evil. Those who are bright and talented not only have an increased ability to birth new realities, but also an increased capacity to birth the reality of destruction. Deception, deviousness, and destruction are enabled more thoroughly through one whose brilliance can create incredible damage. As our intelligence creates more technology, we expand our capacity to destroy at greater levels. Evil persons can now go beyond destruction on individual levels to destruction of the masses and into the death of the Earth. This could not happen without brilliance.

Even more powerful is the soul that has been corrupted by the power of the underworld. There is a darker presence in the universe, a destructive, life-destroying force that can be tapped into through the dark magic of the occult. This underworld is a reality because in order for divinity to exist in its fullest, it must be able to experience the other side — the power of the darkness. Dark magic, occult, life-draining forces exist and who knows better how to utilize this force than a personality and a soul that already has the propensity towards evil? When the corrupted soul along with the corrupted personality combine forces, the presence of evil is apparent. When this being then chooses to get involved with the dark magic of the universe, there is a life-destroying force that is almost beyond human understanding. This magic is often expressed in events that appear to be mystical and spiritual, but which are really techniques of deceit utilized to ensnare persons who are looking for divine signs. Because this force is denied by so many (especially with New Age beliefs that only goodness exists in the universe), it can weave in and around individual souls and groups of souls without being identified for what it is. And if it is not unmasked, evil will corrupt and destroy on an even more terrifying level.

What happens to those in the presence of evil? Already noted is the experience of revulsion, a sickening feeling of often overwhelming proportions. But because evil lies and distorts the truth, one who comes into contact with evil may find confusion, as his own realities become distorted. And as realities become distorted, values begin to change and also may become corrupted as the sense of right and wrong becomes increasingly nebulous. Evil loves to distort and destroy and it has an insatiable pull; to dive into this darkness is a temptation. And if we come into contact with evil, we may succumb to it and be destroyed by it. For evil is not only attracted to people who are vulnerable to its power, but it is also attracted to people who are soulful, because on an unconscious level, evil wants to be brought to the light. Yet in its attraction to goodness, it attempts to consciously extinguish the light in that person — remember that evil wishes to destroy and annihilate goodness and life. So in the presence of such evil, one must not succumb to its call; one must focus on goodness, compassion, light, and love.

This is how one responds to evil — through light, love, strength and courage, compassion and goodness. Yet if one is susceptible to the power of its call, one needs to walk in the other direction. For as we have already learned, being in the presence of evil can draw one into its insidiousness. Yet to walk away from evil, to subvert being corrupted by it, to live through a force that attempts to destroy, to choose to embrace goodness instead, allows the experience of evil to be a transforming one. To survive such an onslaught of insidiousness, one needs a balanced sense of self and divine strength. Indeed, we may call the power of evil to ourselves in order to learn, to heal, to transform, and to utilize our innate divinity to choose the path of goodness. In order to eradicate evil, we must understand it, test it, and reject its power for what it is — the power to destroy life. It is a test of the soul.

To embrace evil in another human being is to do nothing more than accept someone as she is, loving her just as we love someone who is a soulful being, because evil responds to love and to goodness. While this may not provide an immediate transformation in the evil being, it does set a course of opening doors into the energy of the Light, doors that over time may begin to crack open. Although it may take many incarnations for the soul to transform itself and to choose human bodies of lighter energy, the path has been set forth.

And we must never choose hatred as a response to evil, for to hate evil and attempt to destroy it is an evil deed itself. If we attempt to destroy evil, we only destroy ourselves in the process and destroy light energy that may be available to heal, for, "If you strike without compassion against the darkness, you yourself enter the darkness" (Zukav 72).

I have had both professional and personal experiences with evil and these experiences have been both terrifying and transforming. Professionally, I have worked with many perpetrators and victims of childhood sexual abuse. Yet not all perpetrators are evil. Let's examine this further.

A shadow thought could be one of thinking about perpetrating sexual abuse against a young daughter (we will use a male as the perpetrator, although women are also abusers). This may end at just a thought with no action taken. The man having this thought may feel shame over such thinking and he hopefully has the ability to see how destructive this thought is and will not follow through with the behavior. But if he is unable to stop the behavior and acts out on his desire, we see that behavior becomes one of an evil act.

Yet not all evil acts are conducted by evil persons. Evil acts may be conducted by persons who still have light energy, but the light may be dimmed due to addictions, mental illness, misguided beliefs, reenactment of abuse that had been perpetrated on these souls, current trauma and loss, and a number of other states of mind. For example, many years ago I worked with a man who had raped a woman during a psychotic episode. Was he evil? No, he was a sick man whose behavior was evil. He was able to accept responsibility for this rape and was able to feel remorse over his actions and how he traumatized the woman he raped. The ability to feel remorse and accept responsibility is a defining factor regarding whether one has committed an evil act or whether one is actually an evil being. For the lack of compassion is also a symptom of evil beings.

I also worked with a man whose teenage daughter was in substance abuse treatment and while she denied that he was sexually abusing her, staff members were convinced he was. What convinced us? His slippery "feel," the revulsion we felt when around him, the way he watched his daughter and his interaction with her, and her odd, seductive behavior when she was around him. He felt evil to us, but there was nothing to do for her but say prayers as she adamantly denied he was abusive. We had to allow her to return to him. It was a situation that still haunts me.

In my personal life, I have also come in contact with evil persons, some acquaintances, some whom I believed to be friends. And two of these people were practicing psychotherapists, who not only presented a picture of spirituality, but who also presented as recovering from their own issues in order to help others. Such deception is incredibly scary. With the exception of one person, all of them were either involved in church and/or stated they lived a spiritually-filled life. But as I got to know these people, I was filled with horror at the behaviors they perpetrated on others, all the while claiming goodness. The deception, the lies, the cunning, the viciousness of some of their acts, and for two people, the involvement of dark magic, have made this non-believer of evil a believer of such pathology.

One such person was a master of this dark magic, magic that at first appeared to be of goodness and godliness, but which was used as a way to charm and manipulate. This individual had two spirit guides that gave what appeared to be spiritual advice, but which was used against me. She was able to become disembodied as I watched her soul detach from her physical body; she used a child spirit to try to keep me attached to her. She was able to make material objects disappear before my very eyes. This woman was a great manipulator with her lies and emotional abuse. In the end, I believe that she utilized her darkness to try to kill me, to get me to jump out of a car moving at 80 miles-per-hour (I was not suicidal). I soon ended all contact with this person. She is no longer in my life and I wonder whom she is victimizing today.

While I always believed there were evil acts but not evil beings, I am now both a survivor and believer of evil which exists in people and in a further depth of the underworld. As life is a dialectic, both good and evil exist and to deny this is to misunderstand such power in the universe.

The following is an account of an encounter I had with someone that I thought might become a good friend. However, I soon discovered this person to be evil. This is my reaction to such evil.

"Diediediediediediedie." A mantra repeats itself in the incessant chattering of my mind. Yet it's not my mantra, but that of a person who had chosen darkness over lightness. It is her words I hear, words not from her physical presence, but from somewhere within her and which taps into my soul. She is no where near me — miles away on this physical plane, yet within the depths of my being.

What has precipitated this? The end of a budding friendship, a confrontation about her dwindling mental state, a concern that she was slipping into mental illness. Her denial of the situation — slamming the phone down after agreeing to call me later. But somehow I knew I would never hear from her again, for I had found her out and she did not want to be found. I knew that I had lost her as a friend and that she was slipping into the depths of pathology. But I didn't know the extent of the abyss until that evening when I began hearing, "diediedie."

After work that day of the confrontation, I went home and sank into the bathtub to cleanse me of the grime of the day, to wash off the trauma and sorrow that I hear daily as a psychotherapist. But on this evening, cleansing didn't take place as other darkness began to permeate my existence. The chanting began while I was soaking in the tub. I was upset, hurt by the ending of a relationship that I had believed had potential for a positive, spiritual nature. Yet I knew, truly knew, that this relationship was over and that my friend was unwilling and incapable of seeking the help she needed. The pathology that I'd seen in small bouts was now roaring in its evidence. The chanting began and I started to feel overwhelmed with a sorrow I could not express. I didn't want to die; why was I feeling like death was upon me?

Eventually my partner came home from work and found me lying in bed and sobbing without explanation. I tried to explain what was happening, but who can explain the unexplainable? I didn't understand what I was experiencing; I only knew I was feeling suicidal but that these feelings weren't mine (I later discovered that she had a penchant for threatening suicide). Into the evening this continued, into the next few days — a horror of suicidal thoughts, a sense of depersonalization, a trauma of death, and finally, an insight. I was being pulled into the darkness of the woman who had been my friend. And it was a darkness beyond that of one who is experiencing the devastation of a mental illness. It was a darkness of evil and I was its participant — however unwillingly.

My partner was able to walk me through this experience and pull me out of the depths of someone else's hell. For three evenings we went on this journey — I sought to help my friend leave the darkness, but she used the dark magic of the underworld to keep me in this place with her. My partner worked to bring me back to present-time reality and to leave the friend and the darkness behind. It was a mind-boggling experience, one in which my significant other and I had no experience, no mind set to wrap our intellect around in order to place it in some form of understanding.

During the last of these three nights, I was back on the metaphysical plane with my friend and we were in her house. I had only been in her physical house one time previously, but nothing seemed amiss. But it held the secrets of evil and the secrets of the person who had submitted to such a dark force. This I discovered the third night, for on that night, I took this metaphysical journey to her home in order to help her leave this black hole, and to enable her to forsake that which had sucked her into a level of horror. But she refused to come with us. I tried to pull her into the car, to get her to take that first step in saying goodbye to the darkness, but she refused to come. Instead, she tried to seduce me with the delights of the damned, to tempt me with the illusion of beauty and love, to keep me in the hands of devilish darkness. For darkness has an insatiable appetite and it offers itself up to those who are willing to heed that call. My partner and I refused this call. We allowed her to stay in the abyss, for it was her journey and her choice. She remains alive and who knows what darkness she is still suffering. I just hope that she is no longer working as a therapist and perpetrating her evil onto others.

So why am I drawn to such evil? Was it the connection with my friends or are they drawn to me, hoping that on some level I can help them out of their living hell? Or am I too easily seduced by the darkness? What these encounters have done is to help me to develop a level of spiritual connection and understanding that was previously missing, which is not only valuable to my personal spiritual life, but to my life as a therapist as well. I have experienced both heaven and hell.

In our exploration of evil, we must also examine it as a collective. For while evil is expressed through individuals and through the dark underlying presence of the underworld, evil is also magnified in its relationship to groups of persons. While we will not examine group psychology, we must acknowledge that persons may become more corrupt in a group, thereby creating evil on a broader spectrum of existence leading to greater destruction. Studies show that people will become involved in more corruption on a group level because there is a type of "herd" mentality that causes normally sane people to participate in insane actions. Let us explore one example of such evil — the destruction of the World Trade Center in New York City and the resulting destruction of Afghanistan and Iraq through retaliation.

September, 11, 2001 — a day of evil. How does one describe the insidiousness of the terrorist attacks on this day? How does one wrap his intellect around such atrocities and come to a level of understanding? How can one connect to emotions other than horror and terror or find a level of spiritual connection within the darkness? These are the questions of a nation and a universe weeping tears of despair. These are the questions of the Beloved who is crying along with us, who is devastated by what her creation has wrought.

In our horror and our fear, we begin to recognize the level of our own capabilities for destruction. Examine your initial response to the news of this attack. Did you immediately switch into the mode of your own darkness, wanting to annihilate those who had perpetrated such evil? Many of us did. How many instead chose to go into prayer, prayer not just for the people killed and their loved ones, but also for the terrorists and for peace? It is so easy to respond out of our own capabilities for violence. And how has the United States responded?

We heard President George W. Bush continually discuss the evil deeds of the terrorists, but did he acknowledge the evil that the U.S. perpetrates? For to respond to evil with countermeasures of destruction and killing is indeed evil, whether acknowledged or denied. And herein lies the deception of evil — we refuse to admit our own evil deeds, instead convincing a despairing nation that we are healing the world through the battle against terrorism. Have we admitted to ourselves that the people of Afghanistan, Iraq, and many other countries are victims of our terrorism just as much as were those who died in the World Trade Center? When we deny the truth on individual or collective levels, we are perpetuating the process of darkness. This darkness festers and grows and unless brought into the light of reality, will continue to expand into evil, thereby corrupting those who are a part of it — a collective evil.

Are there times we must respond to evil with evil? Perhaps. Perhaps in order to eradicate evil as a collective, we must implement our own evil deeds. Certainly during WWII we focused on eradicating Hitler and the Third Reich, and we did it through destructive means. Yet if we must respond to evil with evil, we need to acknowledge it for what it is, as evil begets evil. If we do evil deeds, we may succumb to becoming evil individuals, evil groups, and evil as a collective. By admitting to the suffering, terror, and death we cause by responding with our own evil deeds, we may save ourselves and the world from sinking into further depths of evil. Perhaps. Perhaps we only delude ourselves into believing this in order to justify our means.

Philosopher Sam Keen articulately describes the problem of evil in the world. He states:

> The most terrible of all the moral paradoxes [. . .] is that we create evil out of our highest ideals and most noble aspirations. We so need to be heroic, to be on the side of God, to eliminate evil, to clean up the world, to be victorious over death, that we visit destruction and death on all who stand in the way of our heroic historical destiny. We scapegoat and create absolute enemies, not because we are intrinsically cruel, but because focusing our anger on an outside target, striking at strangers, brings our tribe

or nation together and allows us to be a part of a close and loving in-group. We create surplus evil because we need to belong. (201-202)

Surplus evil — as though there isn't already enough evil in the world.

I'm weeping the tears of the Beloved,

Divine tears of

blood, gore, starvation, terror, death.

Pungent, odoriferous rotting of

human flesh corrupted by

human souls of evil.

All of us awaiting death,

not of death and rebirth,

but the end of civilization

in a humanity that is annihilating itself.

Weeping your tears;

How you must suffer

is beyond this human's

imaginings.

In the end, what will save us is the healing of our own souls for as we heal individually, we heal collectively. If we do not do our shadow work, if we do not embrace compassion and goodness, if we do not practice honesty in our self assessments, and if we do not trust the Creator with his creation, we will exterminate ourselves and the planet through hatred, cruelty and evil. It is time to give up our narcissistic pride in our individualism and nationalism and work together as a species and as a universe, healing ourselves and others through love and acceptance. And we must all do our part, not relying on someone else to do the work, but to do our inner work individually and to help others in their processes as well. For we are the only enemy and until we understand that, we will not be able to grow beyond our self-imposed limitations into the grace of Goddess. And we can grow into such grace by Being for God.

Part Three:

Being for God

Section Three explores our being for God — not doing — but being. We so often focus on doing and busyness that we seldom tap into the innate joy of being. This section examines our relationship to the Divine through nature, solitude and silence, and living a prayerful life.

Chapter Seven

NATURE AS BLESSING

O Great Spirit
Whose voice I hear in the winds,
and whose breath gives life to all the world,
hear me! I am small and weak, I need your strength
and wisdom.
Let me walk in beauty, and make my eyes
ever behold the red and purple sunset.
Make my hands respect the things you have made
and my ears sharp to hear your voice.
Make me wise so that I may understand the things
you have taught my people.
Let me learn the lessons you have hidden in every
leaf and rock.
I seek strength, not to be greater than my brother,
but to fight my greatest enemy — myself.
Make me always ready to come to you with clean
hands and straight eyes.
So when life fades, as the fading sunset,
my spirit may come to you without shame. (1-19)
Traditional Native American Prayer (Roberts 188)

The love of nature and the cosmos is interspersed with all other aspects of creation, for this Earth and this universe are the beginnings of creation, and therefore, the beginnings of humanity. We are just an iota of the divine word of God bursting forth in human manifestation. As human beings, we are here to share the joy of creation with the Divine, to revel in what has been and continues to be birthed. All the creatures of the universe sing their praises for such divinity; as humans, we must honor, praise, and celebrate such an existence. For nature and the cosmos are here for all to share. In our sharing is our being for God — the being of oneness with the underlying passion of the universe.

For when we talk about "being in nature," we are relating to much more than simply walking, sitting, or playing, although these are types of being themselves. No, we must delve deeper into the meaning of being, for being is a presence of All That Is. Being in nature is experiencing the totality of life for we are all one with the cosmos. We are the trees, the Sun, the stars, the animals, the plants. Our essence is the essence of all life forms. Our being is made up of the atoms of all sentient and non-sentient beings. Dust of my dust, light of my light, we are all one.

In examining creation, we see that this is a story that begins with the awe and mystery of nature in all her glory as expressed by the Earth and the cosmos. All cultures begin and end in story. Story is about origin as well as pre-origin, about the creation of life as a sacred journey. The story of nature is the story of the interrelationship of all beings to the cosmos. The story of nature is about the interrelationship of man and universe, for we were placed here to experience the wonder and mystery of Creator and creation and to co-create in such mysticism.

This Earth story is one that reverberates in the soul. It is a story that transcends time and space and has its origins before its origins. A story that is as unique in its presentation as it is common in the ground of existence; a microcosm of a macrocosm. For this story is unique to each human being and is related to the story of the universe. But so often this story is neglected.

In this story is the underlying genetically coded script including the wisdom of all the ages. This splendor displays itself through the stars and the Moon, the Earth and the water, the plants and the animals. This splendor is an innate feeling, a language of the soul that speaks deep within. This language is a joy-filled connection of human, nature, and cosmos. Somewhere within is the God/Goddess of existence. Somewhere within is the mystery of the story, a mystery that continues to inspire awe and reverence. There is a longing for something greater. There is a connection for what is, has been, and will be. A passion for life — all life; an intimacy with ourselves as well as with all other creatures and with the Beloved. An identity of being in oneness. Who we are, who we were, and who we will be has been and will continue to be expanded into further understanding and further acceptance of the mystery and the mysticism of this incredible cosmos. Life is a gift to be celebrated for all experiences are of a sacred journey; all experiences are story.

On this journey, the story of "I" is no longer a narcissistic story of grandiose proportions but the greater story of who "i am" in relationship to this fascinating cosmological story. How do we fit into the plan of consciousness birthed forth billions of years ago? For humanity must become conscious after so many years of semi-consciousness, and for some of us, unconsciousness. Conscious of the interrelationship of all life and the harmony of unity that we must dance together in order for the planet and the human to survive and eventually thrive in a system that is being destroyed solely (and soul-lessly) by humankind. Cosmologist Brian Swimme and ecologist Thomas Berry tell us:

> There is eventually only one story, the story of the universe.
> Every form of being is integral with this comprehensive story.
> Nothing is itself without everything else. Each member of the
> Earth community has its own proper role within the entire
> sequence of transformations that have given shape and identity
> to everything that exists. (268).

The story of the universe, this story of the creation of the cosmos, is one that must continue to be expanded. We must all work to continue developing this story or it will end in a tragic death, just as the universe itself will cease to exist, or at least, the universe will annihilate those of us in the Earth community who continue to destroy the gifts of the gods and goddesses. So how do we expand this story? We expand it by exploring the history of creation and our ongoing roles in this creation, and by developing a deep intimacy with Gaia and loving it to its core, from the most basic elements to the most complicated forces. And also, by understanding that we are the rocks, trees, sea squirts, and chimps, and that we are not separate from them as we are all one in this blessed life. In this unity of creation, we must celebrate its numinous nature — rejoice in its beauty, praise these divine gifts, and do whatever it takes to save the universe from the destruction of humankind. And each and every person must find his or her own story, for without story, there is no language to express this incredible journey.

Nature must be loved fully to the heights of her spirit and to the depths of her soul. The part that each of us can play is an incredible journey into love and compassion. The beauty of creation, the joy of communing with nature, the cycle of birth/death/rebirth — all allow for a connection that is beyond this physical world and which is of the mystical. Yet within this beauty and pleasure of Earth and cosmos lies the destruction of nature. She destroys not out of a need to harm, but out of a need to change, to expand, and to revitalize. These are the natural laws of the universe. This is a creative act in which death occurs and rebirth follows. Tornadoes, hurricanes, volcanoes, violent storms, blizzards and a myriad of other natural events serve as reminders of the power of this universe. A power that creates, destroys, and recreates. A power that reminds us of our powerlessness. A strength that informs us that we must work together with nature instead of raping her in our belief that more is better and our belief that the material is destiny.

In this universe story of birth/death/rebirth, we find so much beauty, joy, and mystery. Here we learn story as nature, story as man reaching to touch eternity. For how do we reach and touch the Moon? It is not a rhetorical question. For to reach and touch the Moon is to believe that it is possible, that through the blessings of the Divine, we are all one in the harmony of existence.

How did Henry David Thoreau touch the Moon? By living his own story and by immersing himself in the solitude, peace, and love of nature. Listen to his words. "Every morning was a cheerful invitation to make my life of equal simplicity, and I must say innocence, with Nature herself. I have been as sincere a worshipper of Aurora as the Greeks" (64). And, "This is a delicious evening, when the whole body is one sense, and imbibes delight through every pore. I go and come with a strange liberty in Nature, a part of herself" (90). Such beauty Thoreau expresses through the word of nature, the story of creation, the prose of God.

For me, this is the song of the morning — the dawn of creation in her glory of sunshine, the morning doves cooing their joy, the wind whipping the summer breeze with the fresh air perfume of Northern Michigan, and the waves of the lake lapping upon the shore while the gulls, ducks, and geese verbalize their heart songs. For creation is the silence of a snowstorm, the pine trees swaying in a thunderstorm, the breathtaking air of newly plowed farmland, and the full moon reflecting off the lake. These are the ongoing expressions of the soul of the universe, the soul which reaches into our own souls in a manifestation of the love of the Beloved. This is divinity manifest where immanence meets transcendence.

Infuse me, oh Ra,

with your plethora of rays,

of peacock feathers

glowing in the aftermath

of irradiated light energy.

Take away my gift of sight

so that I might see.

Bathe me in the waters

awash with the power of

Triton to heal me from all

the wounds of unrequited love.

For you are the light, the gift,

the focus of my madness

steeped in divine bliss

soaking my entire being

for all the world to see.

Kiss me Ra and take me to your limit.

Creation began as a journey of light and darkness, this creative genesis of the universe. The energy at the dawn of existence is a mystical quality of all that is of time, light, space, and creativity. This energy of the
cosmos includes the earthiness of creation for fecundity is the ultimate act
of creativity. In our connection to the Earth and the heavens, we explore the
passion of whom and what we are in our sensuality. This taste of all existence, the heaven of above and below, is felt through our senses. Our senses
and our sensuality are fully expressed in nature. In our genetically encoded
scripts, we recognize that we are the Sun, the sand, and the stars. For we
were created in the birth of the stars and the particles that were formed out
of such birth. We are living nature and our dust is nature itself. L. Robert
Keck discusses this as related to the "Big Bang" theory, noting that,
"Everything in the universe apparently started in a unity, is one indivisible
whole, and the whole is simply expanding" (149). The past, the present,
and the future of the universe are related. Our breath is the breath of the
Beloved. We are one with all creatures, all planets, all of the cosmos.

The Earth and cosmos keep us alive through the ongoing love of the
interaction of human to divine. To be humble within the glory of God is to
drink in the earthiness and the sensuality of life. For earthiness and sensuality are the connections to oneself, to Gaia, the universe, and the Divine
Creator. Connecting with creation is creative itself; it is listening, touching,

hearing, smelling, and tasting the life divine. These are the sacred moments of awe, blessing, and being blessed.

In our story, in the birthing of creation, through the sensuality and the mystery, we must bless all that has been given. The Beloved has created such an incredible display of divinely endowed beauty. All has been blessed. From the smallest cell to the largest killer whale, from the plants to the planets, from the fishes and the seas, all is of grace and must be honored. We need to be open to this ecstasy, this pleasure, this joy of life. For in the reverence is the blessing.

To bless is to be involved, to be fully connected to self and to all that has been gifted, to see Goddess in what has been birthed. To savor this beauty and this expansiveness, to pleasure oneself through connecting to Earth and cosmos is to be not only divinely blessed, but to be a blessing. This is the blessing of awe. What a totality — this Earth and universe! The strength of the divine word as expressed in nature overcomes us. Each and every expression of the mystery of nature is blessed. For we learn that even the peskiest mosquito has been birthed in love and delight and is a gift of the Beloved. Who are we to deny it life merely because it annoys us?

I have always been connected to the joys of nature. As a child, I loved exploring the woods and creek around the family home, riding on the tractor or combine with my father, gathering bittersweet with my grandmother, watching the tadpoles grow, finding arrowheads, and viewing the heron that visited the swamp. How unfortunate that so many people grow up without having the blessing of nature in their lives and who miss this connection with the universe, this awe of the Divine.

We so often deny these blessings in our search for life's meaning. How often we overlook these daily delights in our struggle for power and control, in our attempts to run from our divinity, in our busyness, in our addictions. We are the co-creators of the ending of our story; what will be this ending? For if we don't expand our story into the awe, beauty, and mystery of creation, and if we persist in our patriarchal, hierarchical, Earth-and-body raping, misogynistic, racist, homophobic, religiously persecuting, and nationalistic ways, the story will end in total destruction, total annihilation of this gift of creation.

So how do we change this ending? In our original blessing we see that everything in life is to be revered, from that obnoxious mosquito to the glory of the sunrise. We must expand upon our story — for we grow story and story grows us if we so allow it. This sacred experience is restored through the word of God, the earthiness of both heaven and Earth, the beauty of the universe, and the blessing given and received by creation. This is the praise of God, both in the giving and in the receiving. As Carol Christ notes, "Knowledge that we are but a small part of life and death and transformation is the essential religious insight. The essential religious response is to rejoice and to weep, to sing and to dance, to tell stories and create rituals in praise of an existence far more complicated, more intricate, more enduring than we are" (321).

Finally, let us turn to the wisdom of Hildegard of Bingen, who in her writings reveals the poetry of the interrelationship of human and nature. She expresses the wisdom of all the ages. This is nature as blessing and nature as being. Let us celebrate such loveliness.

With nature's help,

humankind can set into creation

all that is necessary and life sustaining.

God's majesty is glorified

in the manifestation of every manner

of nature's fruitfulness.

This is possible,

possible through the right and holy

utilization of the earth,

the earth in which humankind has its

source.

The sum total of heaven and earth,

everything in nature,

is thus won to use and purpose.

It becomes a temple and altar

for the service of God. (1 - 16)

                                            (Uhlein 107)

Chapter Eight

OF SOLITUDE AND SILENCE

To Enjoy This Conversation

Make everything in you an ear, each atom of your being, and you will hear at every moment what the Source is whispering to you, just to you and for you, without any need for my words or anyone else's. You are — we all are — the beloved of the Beloved, and in every moment, in every event of your life, the Beloved is whispering to you exactly what you need to hear and know. Who can ever explain this miracle? It simply is. Listen and you will discover it every passing moment. Listen, and your whole life will become a conversation in thought and act between you and Him, directly, wordlessly, now and always.

It was to enjoy this conversation that you and I were created.

Rumi (Harvey 99)

Solitude and silence — states of being that enable us to seek and attain closer communion with Goddess. To enter this state of connection with the Divine, we need to submerge into the quietness to hear her voice, for that is where she lies. In this communion we let be, trusting in the innate quiet and emptiness of the soul of our being. For the Beloved is within and without and we can reach her if we stop the inner and outer noise. The soul revitalizes in silence and aloneness. It is nurtured, refreshed, and expanded in these empty places.

And these empty places, these places of stillness, can be of loneliness or of aloneness as both states exist for us to learn and to grow into our divinity. Loneliness is a sense of sadness, a longing for connection to other persons, to nature, to the cosmos, and to Goddess. Loneliness is a sense of emptiness, a nothingness which longs to be filled, but which enriches our lives in its void. Yet too often loneliness is thought of only in a negative light — to be lonely is to be isolated, often in a state of gloom and despair over the solitary existence. And so we frequently rush into action, taking steps to try to fill this emptiness through relationships, sex, food, drugs, busyness, work, and whatever else might darn the hole. Yet our loneliness allows us to reach the depths of nothingness, to sit in silence and accept that this emptiness, this void, this shell of existence, is for our benefit. We may suffer through this loneliness, and in our suffering, we can choose to heal or choose to destroy ourselves with petty concerns. All works of loneliness are good works which offer us opportunities to reach into the depths of our humanity and our divinity.

For while loneliness is a human experience of the ego, it is also a heart experience of the soul. We've all known the human aspect of loneliness, feeling unloved and missing the intimacy of family and friends. But do we understand the depths of the loneliness of the soul? Here we find that empty place which only the Beloved can fill; here we find that nothingness that is so necessary to reach the depths of creation. Yet how utterly terrifying to feel this emptiness. It is so much deeper than the simple longing for companionship on the level of the personality.

But if we can sit back and allow loneliness to be and to do nothing about it, we can come to terms with the very emptiness of existence. And in accepting this core of loneliness, we begin to transform our fears of solitude into the acceptance of aloneness. This is how we shall define solitude for the rest of our journey — solitude is being able to delight in aloneness, aloneness being the capacity to be with oneself. Healthy solitude is accepting the intimacy you have with yourself and with God. In solitude, we learn who we are and what we are — divine beings. We heal ourselves on the level of the personality and the psyche. For the *"capacity to be alone thus becomes linked with self-discovery and self-realization; with becoming aware of one's deepest needs, feelings, and impulses"* (italics by author, Storr 21). In solitude, we are offered wisdom and knowledge, and we grow into our creativity. The capacity to embrace solitude is a capacity of the emotionally and spiritually healthy individual who seeks this aloneness as a time of joy and a time of sorrow.

In our solitude, we learn we are never truly alone for we are always in the presence of the Beloved. In our aloneness, we grow and expand our human self, but more importantly, we expand our understanding and acceptance of our divine self. In such aloneness, we learn to befriend ourselves and revel in such compatibility. We also seek the companionship we have with the Beloved, for it is often within solitude that we calm ourselves enough to feel the blessings within and without.

So how do we learn to embrace solitude? First, we begin by teaching it to our children and by being role models to them. To teach that solitude and loneliness are nothing to fear, but something to celebrate. To teach so that we too, can learn that it is a healing process. We teach by allowing them time alone in school and at home. We teach by talking about how they can find their deepest selves through such silence and through using their imagination and creativity. We teach there is fullness in life through such silence instead of allowing them to spend hours on mind-numbing TV and computer games.

In their solitude, children learn to explore themselves and the world around them. They learn to befriend themselves and to explore their imagination. They learn to listen to their inner guides, those innate voices that soothe and teach. And they learn they are never alone, no matter what their here-and-now reality is.

Much of my childhood was spent in aloneness as we lived on a farm and I had no nearby friends. My brothers are five and seven years older than me and had their own interests, although we did spend a lot of time together playing sports. My father was a farmer, school bus driver, and carpenter who worked long hours, and my mother was depressed and wasn't often available. So I learned how to be alone. I spent hours in the woods with my dog, Arfie (and who is ever alone in the company of a beloved pet), reading and drawing, playing catch with myself — all solitary activities. Although at times I was lonely, I was able to adapt and embrace such solitude. I discovered my love of nature and all her creatures. Although I didn't understand it at the time, this was where my spiritual connection developed. I discovered the joys of reading and fantasy, and I embraced doing art work and began my own creative process. Do I ever regret the loneliness I felt at times? No, for I have found that through such times, I learned to delve into the spirituality of solitude, and the beauty and oneness of creation.

In embracing solitude for ourselves, we must let go of fear, under-standing that while we may feel scared of its emptiness, it does not wish to harm, but only to help us journey into our own depths. And herein lies faith: faith that we are truly never alone, faith that we can enter and exit solitude as we please, faith that a divine power is there to carry us over the threshold of our fear. That we admit to our fear and still walk through it is a testament to our faith, allowing solitude to open us to new worlds of spir-itual connections. As we learn to desire solitude, we expand to an openness of the peace of its very existence and in this peace we discover and redis-cover God. "And I could see how simple it is to find God in solitude," relates mystic Thomas Merton. "There is no one else, nothing else. He is all there is to find there. Everything is in Him. And what could be more pleasing to Him than that we should leave all things and all company to be with Him and think only of Him and know Him alone, in order to give Him our love?" (28).

In solitude, we discover the silence of being. In patience and endurance, we await that still small voice of Beloved calling us home. And she does call — through love and compassion — she awaits us just as we await her. She is always there, lovingly embracing us. Yet how seldom we heed this call. Only through our aloneness, our emptiness, and our silence, do we receive these messages of God.

These mysteries come through the silence of the peace and quiet understanding of the soul. Silence can be internal and external, immanent and transcendent. It is the sound of serenity, the emptiness of being, and the sense of nothingness. It is the sound of nature, of cherubim whispering, of the universe humming. Silence is the peace of stillness, a quieting within the humanness to reach the divineness. To live in silence is an act of strength. To be able to calm the mind chatter, to tune out the noise of the world, to sink into the depths of quietude, is an act of the soul. For the soul revitalizes in silence and in solitude. It is refreshed and nurtured through this state of being. Through our heart, we empty into the stillness of exis-tence, as only by emptying the heart can the Divine fully reveal herself in all her essence. This emptying of the heart is the opening to the soul.

In the quiet, we learn to free ourselves from the false ego self which has imprisoned us through its limited human existence. The ego which has dimmed the light of the soul through its overbearing dominance has kept us trapped from the connection to the Beloved. This is running away from our true nature, our essential self, because we are so afraid of who and what we are. We must go through the annihilation of this false self, the ego which presents itself with a mask of deception, hiding our true identity and the truth of our being. This death of the ego is so difficult, so painful, that it may feel as though one is stepping off the face of the Earth into the depths of hell. But the reality is that through this process, one enters fully into the entire universe, the cosmos of all light and love — the Beloved. From the dark womb of our existence, we die and are reborn into the silence of the Goddess.

Yet for many of us, silence was dangerous and the ego is all that we had to protect us. Perhaps we were raised in families where the rule was, "don't talk, don't trust, don't feel," so that keeping silent was keeping the sickness of the family hidden. We learned that silence was related to dysfunction and so as adults, silence may frighten us. How scary to go back into silence after years of being forced into silence; how terrifying to try to find health and wholeness that can be acquired in the stillness. And for others, we were silenced because we were children, we were women, we were minorities. In essence, we were the silent majority — the unseen, the unloved, the downtrodden in a society that didn't honor our very being. Who then would listen to our voices? Who would hear our secrets, share our fears, and delight in our victories? Silence was so lonely, so hurtful, so empty.

In the capacity as a therapist, I hear how the rule of "don't talk, don't trust, don't feel," has caused so much damage to the spirit. Being silenced —whether verbally, physically, emotionally, sexually, or spiritually — causes such trauma. For if there is no voice, there is no way to express the pain, the trauma, and the hurt. And without a voice, the joy, fun, and reverence are also silenced, for we must be able to express our emotions in order to be fully connected to our spirit. Therapy is a way to give voice to this traumatic silence.

Yet for some of us to go beyond the traumas of our lives, we need to learn to live in our own silence and to touch the emptiness and the pain. While grieving may take place with the help of others, the soul of healing resides in solitude and silence. In this quiet we find our joy, passion, sorrow, delight, pain, and creativity. We learn to trust and honor the Beloved in this space. Through the hubbub of our everyday rush of life, Spirit is there calling us forth. When will we gather the strength to be alone in the solitude and stillness to listen to her wisdom?

For silence is not just a gift of the Beloved, but is the Beloved. In the quietness, we gift ourselves with his love; an emptying in order to fully expand into grace. To sink into this silence is to trust, fully trust, the Divine with no illusions, no expectations, no thoughts, and no beliefs. To delve into the soul in order for God to appear is to listen to the quiet.

Mystic Meister Eckhart indicates that, "'you have to divest yourself of all your activities and bring all your powers to silence if you really wish to experience this birth within yourself'" (Fox 257). In this death of the self, the stillness, the emptiness, the nothingness, allow God to enter you in order to fill you. To fill you with the love that only he can provide, for in this silence you will be blessed with the word of God and transformed into the rebirth of self. In this silence, we hear the word of the One for when we are in such stillness, our nothingness turns into the something-ness. This is the word that reverberates in the soul, the individual soul, which allows us to expand into the depths of all of creation. For silence is of creation; all of life begins and ends in silence.

Yet how do we stop the noise of our everyday lives? There is an over-abundance of such sound in our lives. There is the noise within our own minds, that often endless chattering which distracts us from the Source. We hear the noise of the sounds of people constantly doing. And while there are sounds in silence, these are the sounds of Creation, from the still-ness of the wind to the beating of your heart. The plethora of joyful, heal-ing, loving sounds of the Earth and cosmos embrace us if we just listen to them hum. These sounds are the prayers of the Creator.

In examining our solitude and silence, we turn to the work of Evelyn Underhill who discusses the need for contemplation and the withdrawal from the outer world in order to enter the inner world of God. This is a soli-tary process in which the soul is expanded. In turning within, we enter a state of introversion. To enter this communion we utilize what is described as mystical prayer — orison — which, "In some of its degrees it is a placid, trustful waiting upon messages from without. In others, it is an inarticulate communion, a wordless rapture, a silent gazing upon God" (306).

Underhill further relates that this relationship with God is reached through Recollection, Quiet, and Contemplation in this process of intro-version. In our silence, we enter into Recollection often through medita-tion. This is a beginning step in which we begin to clear out the busyness of our everyday lives. Through meditation we may utilize a sacred word, name, or prayer in order to begin opening the soul to higher realms of con-nection.

Through Recollection, we begin to train ourselves in the practice of contemplation and through these meditative experiences, we then enter into the Prayer of Quiet, that silence in the depth of the interior self. This is a surrendering to the inflowing God where consciousness of the sensuous world melds into the consciousness of the Beloved. In the Quiet, we allow God to speak and we must be receptive to her voice. There is a peace of understanding, a sense of humility that we enter through this stage, which further opens the door into the next stage, Contemplation, which is the state of furthering the human/Divine connection. And there are two seemingly paradoxical conditions that are experienced within Contemplation, although in reality, they are dialectical experiences, a both/and relationship. This is so beautifully described by Underhill:

> The contemplative self who has attained this strange country can only tell an astonished and incredulous world that here his greatest deprivation is also his greatest joy; that here the extremes of possession and surrender are the same, that ignorance and knowledge, light and dark, are One. Love has led him into that timeless, spaceless world of Being which is the peaceful ground, not only of the individual striving spirit, but also of the striving universe [. . .]. (339)

This is the transcendent state, the mystical union, the ultimate connection of human and divine, realized through the solitude and silence of everyday existence. This is the merging into the Beloved; the death of the ego self into the completeness of the divine self. In this merging, the "I" of our personhood melds into the "We" of All That Is. While this is the merging of human/divine, we recognize that we are merely finding the divinity which is already present.

Yet our connection with the Beloved need not always be complicated. How often do we hear that inner voice when we sit and listen, simply, quietly listen? All states, from simple listening, to beginning meditation and prayer, and to the deeper states of union with Grace, are divine states which bless us if we so allow them. We need silence to hear the voice within; that inner wisdom provided through the emptiness.

As previously discussed, I have spent many hours of my life in the silence, beginning in childhood. Today, I still spend a lot of time in silence -- on my float or swimming in the perfect blue waters of northern Michigan, walking in the woods and along the shoreline, meditating and praying, planting my garden, watching a snow storm while basking in the warmth of my fireplace, and simply watching the trees bend in the summer breeze. In this silence, I have clearly heard and felt the words of Yahweh whispered in my ears, a loving voice which guides me to a deeper connection to All That Is. This silence is a gift I will continue to cherish throughout this lifetime. It is a gift that is as innate to me as is breathing. This is the joy of connection to creation.

In the silence of the garden of creation,

You gave rise to this human manifestation

of divinity.

Lifetime after lifetime I have awaited you.

I await you today.

To birth me into the essence of you,

Where no words are spoken and no sounds

are heard,

Except the utter silence of whispered love.

In the silence,

I adore you,

I await you.

In the silence. . . .

These whispers of the Beloved that come in solitude and in silence lead us into a level of transformation for the individual soul as well as for the collective soul. We have been brought to this planet and into this lifetime in order to seek our divine connection to the Universe. And in such divine connection, we relate to life through prayerful living, a continuation of our being.

Chapter Nine

BOUNTIFUL LIVING: LIFE AS PRAYER

They Continue at Their Prayers

Prayer is not just for the set times of kneeling and bowing; the real challenge of prayer is to prolong that state of absorption always, to keep the heart in a constant blaze of adoration whether you are asleep or awake, writing or reading. In all circumstances and every situation, see that you never wander from God's hand. What is said in the Koran, "They continue at their prayers," should also describe you.

Rumi (Harvey 156)

Living life as prayer is not about praying, although it can be. Living a prayerful life is so much more — it is living life to the fullest, embracing life as a spiritual journey. A prayerful life is steeped in the mysticism and the awe of the sacred. Each and every moment is revered in its sacredness. Each and every moment is honored for the lessons that are provided. When we ponder life as prayer, we often get wrapped up in questions such as: How do we pray? For whom do we pray? What do we pray for? This, however, is placing a limitation on prayer and therefore, on life.

Let us look at a definition of prayer as offered by physician Larry Dossey. He defines prayer as:

> [. . .] petition, asking something for one's self, and intercession, asking for something for others. There also are prayers of confession, the repentance of wrongdoing and the asking of forgiveness; lamentation, crying in distress and asking for vindication; adoration, giving honor and praise; invocation, summoning the presence of the Almighty; and thanksgiving, offering gratitude. (5)

If we take all of these definitions together, we see that everything is prayer; our very essence is prayer. Our being is prayer; our doing is prayer. For in our daily lives, we ask for something for ourselves and for others; we confess to our sins and ask for forgiveness; we cry and scream in our pain and sorrow asking to be vindicated; we honor and praise ourselves, others, and the universe as well as the Beloved. And we call upon the Divine for help and offer our thanks for all of our blessings. In such manner, prayer is all inclusive of these daily nuances of living. If we are fully awake, if we are committed to God, we pray constantly. Prayerfulness is about keeping our heart open to any experience. Whether we pray alone or with others, praying is being for God for it allows us to go to the heart; this heart is where she resides.

If we expand prayer into prayerfulness, we see that life is related to the connections of the soul. For the soul functions in expansiveness, in the union of human to divine, and in the mysticism of daily experiences. And prayer is the language of the soul. It may be silent or it may burst forth in a song or in a dream. It may be danced with joy or drawn in tears. But prayer is always expressive; it is about the soul living the life divine.

Living a prayerful life is living a life of open communion with the Universal Life Force, be it of God or Goddess, Allah or Brahman, the Way or a Higher Power, the Essence or the All, The Divine or the Beloved, the Great Spirit or Krishna. This is the communion of the heart to its very essence. Prayerful living is ultimately being for the Absolute and allowing him the openness of our own divine nature.

In a prayerful life, we ask these questions daily: Did I live life as prayer today? Did I see the divinity in everyone and the world around me? If not, how did I fall short of such prayerfulness? For to live this life divine is to first be awakened to what such a life is and how to conduct it accordingly. Awareness is being awake to everything that surrounds us and is us. Awareness is to be mindful of this incredible experience called living.

What is the essence of living life as prayer? We begin this journey with the experience of awe, wonder, and beauty — the underlying guiding principles of the cosmos, and therefore, of the Beloved. In such fascination, we recognize the beauty of life, pure life, in all its shapes and colors. There is a magical connection to All That Is, an enchantment with what stands before us. Such wonder is the beauty of nature; the awe of our physical bodies; the joy of the interconnection of the living and the dying; the fascination of what we see, feel, taste, touch, and hear. This is embracing life to its fullest.

Yet how seldom do we experience such reverence. How seldom do we participate mindfully in the wonder that surrounds us. We must learn to pay attention to that which enters our earthly and cosmic surroundings. And we can learn to imbibe upon such treasures for that is why we are here.

In such awe and beauty, we discover our passion for living, our passion for being a human essence on this magical playground of the Earth and sea. This is the eros of fully experiencing and expressing the divine nature of ourselves; the scintillating sensuality that is the basis of our human/divine self. This is the joy, ecstasy, and pleasure that we are meant to experience, for as the universe is passionate, so are the Creator and the created. Yet passion involves all the emotions, the suffering and the grief, the longing and the emptiness, the desire and the despair, the fear and the love. Experiencing our emotions is passionate and being fully alive to the wonder of existence.

Prayerful living is also experienced in the mystery and the mysticism of our being. This is the experience of oneness, of the totality of the communion with a Higher Presence. This is of the sacred — where human and divine meet in wonder and in transcendence. It is the ability to accept the unknown, to follow our intuition, to commune with the Source, to resonate with the innate spiritual truths through letting go and letting be. This may happen through prayer, meditation, contemplation, yoga, in silence and solitude, with others — through any experience that leads to the Beloved.

In our prayerfulness, we honor the deep abiding wisdom that guides and heals. For in our reverence wisdom lies. In our gratefulness, our gratitude, our humility, we go beyond the limited ego into the higher self of divine wisdom, divine love, divine being. What an honor to be gifted with such fellowship. We praise, give thanks, and bless all that we have received, all that we are receiving, and all that we will receive. We are graced in love and acceptance through such heartfelt thanksgiving.

In our divine living, we recognize that faith underlies all prayerfulness. Faith in a divine power, faith in the mysticism of our sacred being, faith in ourselves, and faith in all that surrounds us. Faith transcends every level of human pride, ego, and fear. It is living life as prayer and understanding that all is well even in the midst of turmoil. Prayerfulness does not exist without faith.

In my role as therapist, much of the work clients do is based on faith -- however faith is defined by them. We explore the need for hope in our lives and how this hope is what keeps us living. Some people come into therapy with just a thread of hope and we examine this thread and how to strengthen it. We also explore gratitude because by the time many people come into therapy, it is due to crises. Within crises, it is often difficult to find gratitude so clients are given the assignment of listing their gratitudes. Sometimes the list is short, perhaps the only gratitude is that the suicide attempt failed, but we focus upon this as a thread of hope and we go on. Therapy is about examining fear vs. faith and how to grow through this dialectic.

I worked with one young woman who had made a serious suicide attempt by overdosing on medications and drinking on top of this. She was told she probably would not live due to the liver damage from this attempt. She stayed in the Intensive Care Unit for a few days until she came into therapy. By this time, she had been able to explore this attempt and her fear of dying. Many times when people come to consciousness after the suicide attempt, their first response is one of anger because they are still alive.

Yet this was a woman who had done some deep soul-searching and was able to talk about her gratitude to God for keeping her alive. Part of her therapy focused on this spiritual awakening and she was able to begin healing. She saw her purpose in life and the direction she needed to go. I hope she's continued on this path.

We need to continue to awaken to the blessings before us. As we become more awakened, the more everything in our life becomes a prayer. We begin to pray without interruption, pray without ceasing, pray every moment. As we go upon our day, our every moment, every action, and every thought is prayerful. Brother Steindl-Rast states:

> But even for us, it is never too late to recover that prayerfulness which is as natural to us as breathing. The child within us stays alive. And the child within us never loses the talent to look with the eyes of the heart, to combine concentration with wonderment, and so to pray without ceasing. (46)

To pray without ceasing is to live life to its fullness. We must learn to maintain this inner attitude in order to delve into living life as prayer. Living a prayerful life is returning blessing for blessing; it is being for Goddess and it is the beginning transformation into doing for Goddess. It is our destiny.

Here I am.

Take me as I am —

with all the emotional baggage,

with the hurt, pain, and abandonment.

It's not much,

but it's what I have to offer.

Will you accept me as I am?

I want to come home;

Heal me to the depths of my being.

Part Four:

Doing for God

Doing for God is placing our blessings into action in order to help transform and heal not only our individual selves, but the collective self. Part Four relates the importance of compassion, creativity, and service and justice-making in such transformation.

<u>**Chapter Ten**</u>

A MANDALA OF COMPASSION

All sentient beings should be looked upon as equal. On that basis, you can gradually develop genuine compassion for all of them. It must be said that genuine compassion is not like pity or a feeling that others are somehow lower than yourself. Rather, with genuine compassion you view others as more important than yourself.

The Dalai Lama (*Compassion* 64)

In our search for the Beloved, we find that compassion which is of her and of ourselves. We begin by defining compassion and then examining the interrelationship of five types of compassion through a mandala of healing. Through this circle of life, we come to understand that each and every area of life relates to one another and that movement in one area impacts movement in another. This dynamic nature of compassion consists of: 1) the underlying compassion of the universe, 2) love of self, 3) compassion towards others, 4) love of the Earth and cosmos, and 5) union with the Beloved. These forms of compassion are birthed at any time at any level, but tend to begin with the compassion of the universe, and moving clockwise, weave in and out of one another forming a mandala for all of existence.

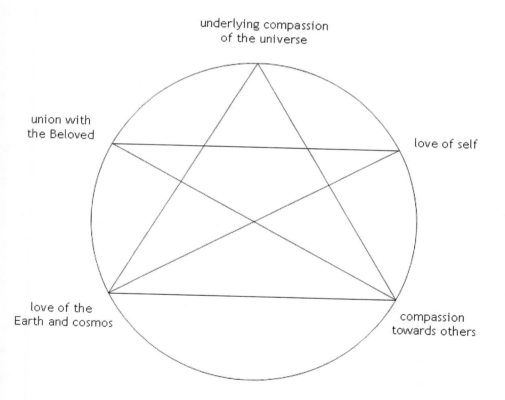

Through this exploration we learn that, "The universe is a sacred marriage between God and matter, spirit and flesh, an entirely sacred holy emanation of divine love; the destiny of human life is to live this sacred marriage here on earth, with as complete and compassionate a consciousness as possible" (Harvey 15).

Compassion is about our heart. The heart is our feeling level connection — feelings of and for ourselves, feelings for others, and the connectedness of our soul with another soul as well as with the universal soul. The heart reveals the aliveness of a being, the ability to be open to love, joy, and compassion, as well as pain and sorrow; the ability to experience the full self. We attach to one another, to life itself, through our heart.

Underlying compassion is reverence and passion. What is reverence? Reverence is the response to the numinousity of life, the sacredness of creation herself. It is that overwhelming feeling one gets when experiencing life at its fullest, whether it is the birth of a child, the death of a loved one, connecting with nature, or loving someone to her core. It is the divine connection of both immanence and transcendence. Reverence cannot be fully defined; mere words regarding the sensation do a disservice to the largeness of the experience. Reverence transforms by its sheer power; how can one not be inspired by overlooking the Grand Canyon, by walking in the woods on a sunny spring day or by listening to beautiful music? Unless we have reverence, we cannot have compassion. To have compassion is to be able to feel the existence of another's pain and suffering, and to have the strength to do something about that suffering. If we are not connected to this awe of existence, we cannot have the compassion or passion to heal ourselves and others.

Passion — the very basis of the word is about suffering, especially the suffering of Christ. To live in passion is to be willing to experience agony and crucifixion; to care so deeply that we will go through any process, no matter what the pain. Current meaning is related to feeling the depths of any emotion — joy, love, sorrow, fear, excitement — to feel intensely. In order to grow and heal, passion must be present in order to lead us to action; to feel so deeply about something or someone that we lovingly respond.

Through our awe and passion, we work to relieve the suffering of others by means of justice-making. Justice-making is our compassion in action; without it, compassion would be nothing but complacency. And with a compassionate heart, we celebrate all that has been provided and we give praise to the Beloved.

THE UNDERLYING COMPASSION OF THE UNIVERSE

In the beginning was compassion; underlying all compassion was (and is) the compassion of the universe. We are birthed into love and compassion, created by the Ultimate Creator in an energetic force of joy, awe, and passion. The love of self, love towards others, compassion with the Earth and cosmos, and union with the Beloved would not exist without this universal blessing of compassion that is our origin. In this mystical union of heart to heart, spirit to spirit, soul to soul, we understand that we are divinely related. For in exploring this Earth and cosmos, it is impossible to not see how we have been birthed in love and joy. All creatures, the planets, the stars and the Sun, the human and the Divine, are blessed and being blessed in this ongoing life energy. What incredible delights Goddess has manifested in our birthright; such a wellspring of divinity. All we must do is open our eyes to the beauty and the awe of what surrounds us in order to embrace this compassionate universe.

Through this life journey, we connect with the sensuality and ecstasy of all of existence and recognize the perfection of life, even within its imperfections. In the understanding of our birthright, we praise, bless, and give thanks for this existence of divine grace and divine love. We celebrate this compassionate universe by continuing to birth new realities as a God-given source of creation. For through celebration we return blessing to the Beloved as she has blessed us. We honor this fecund universe and her love and compassion, for compassion is that part of love which allows for sorrow and pushes us into action.

Brian Swimme explores this compassion by noting that, "love is a word that points to this alluring activity in the cosmos. This primal dynamism awakens the communities of atoms, galaxies, stars, families, nations, persons, ecosystems, oceans, and stellar systems. Love ignites being" (49). We must join this system of universal wonder and love to be able to go beyond, to go beyond and achieve our purpose of existence — to be compassionate beings. To connect with the passion and the purpose of life, to heal ourselves and others, and to continually birth and rebirth is to honor and revere the blessing of life. We can become a part of this creation through our own awakenings, through our efforts to love ourselves.

LOVE OF SELF

An awakened world acknowledges the need for our love of self. By knowing the truth of our own existence, we can begin to transform the self love into the love of others. This is not a narcissistic, unhealthy love of self, but the love of self that is provided by the Divine. Before we can act in compassion with others, we must first act in compassion with ourselves. To love ourselves to our very core — the lightness and darkness of our souls — is a necessity in this human existence. God created us to love ourselves as he loves us, totally, thoroughly, by leaps and bounds, to the inner resources of our being. With total acceptance of our perfections and imperfections; with joy, abundance, and pleasure at what has been birthed. Until we can embrace ourselves as Goddess embraces us, we will remain stuck in an existence of limitation. A limitation of the awesomeness of who and what we are, divine essences of the Source.

As previously discussed, the healthy individual seeking self-actualization has a strong self, an ego strength that allows him to cope with life on life's terms. An awakened individual has self-knowledge, self-love, and self-identity that are born of strength. There is an acceptance of life, an acceptance of strength and weakness, failure and success. The healthy individual experiences pain, pleasure, and desire; relishes the eros of life; connects to nature; and is attached to others. This is an ego in which the mind and heart (i.e., compassion) are open in order to feel, experience, and grow. Dr. Charlotte Kasl states, "*A healthy ego is flexible, porous, open to input, compassionate, and works in the service of goodness. It is a central core within us that allows us to rest firmly in the center of our wisdom and strength*" (italics by author, 59).

Loving ourselves means embracing each and every aspect, including those disowned parts, the pieces of ourselves that we don't accept, whether it is our physical body, our sexuality, our character traits, or our feelings. By learning to accept life as it is and by being compassionate towards everything we are, we can heal from individual concerns such as depression, anxiety, addictive behaviors, and problematic health conditions. And through this healing of ourselves, we can then learn to expand into healing other areas of life.

Within the healthy ego structure we are not separate. In order to fully understand there is no separation, we must have the ego strength to let go of these illusions of separateness, knowing that we are One. The individual who loves herself loves herself through the strength of an underlying divine presence. Compassion is of the Divine; to become a fully compassionate individual, one must have the sense of the divinity both within and without. This is reaching humanity's fullest potential.

Although compassion, an innate God-given quality, may underlie all persons, it often is not fully birthed until we go through our own individual pain and suffering. We may feel the pangs of compassion lurking within our souls, but most often, it takes an act of suffering to render our compassion to its true depths. We must allow pain to be pain and suffering to be suffering in order to transform.

Through suffering, we learn patience, endurance, and acceptance. Suffering teaches us that we are strong and resilient. It teaches us to be compassionate with ourselves, others, and all of life. We learn that there is an underlying strength, the strength of a divine presence that carries us through the depths of our pain. We learn a new level of trust, a faith in the Divine as well as divine faith (that faith that is innate within us, but a faith which sometimes is overlooked). Our suffering provides us with a sense of wisdom as we learn new realities about ourselves and the world around us. We offer our bodies, our spirits, and our souls knowing that in this cosmic reality of love and compassion, we will survive and eventually thrive once again. And we go on.

We must remember in our love of self that we celebrate the self. As human beings, we are awe-inspired and awe-some. The self was created by the Beloved out of grace and holiness. This celebration is of holiness and (w)holiness for we are wholly complete beings in such faith.

A former client of mine was female by sex, masculine by gender. She was heavy set, dressed in men's clothes, and did not comply with the social norms of gender roles. She struggled in finding her way in the world; however she and her female partner had been together about five years. Over time, she began to feel how constraining this lifestyle was for her, as she had always felt the masculine gender was her true gender, not the one she was ascribed at birth. So in her love of herself, she decided to honor herself by transitioning from a female to a male. She began to describe herself as male (she had already taken up the masculine gender role), and began the medical procedures, including hormonal treatments, to help her look more masculine. Facial hair developed and she was looking more like a traditional male. This was a major step in loving who she was and loving her inner self enough to honor its desire.

As we are awakened individually through reverence and passion, through pain and suffering, through delight and celebration, we can then heed the call to respond to the suffering of others as well as the suffering of the planet, the cosmos, and the Source. We answer the call to love and heal on immanent and transcendent levels. As M. Scott Peck tells us:

> Let us prepare ourselves. Let us do so by relearning how important we are, how beautiful we are, and how we are desired beyond our wildest imaginings. And let us, as best we can, go out into the world to teach others how important they are, how beautiful they are, and how they too are desired beyond their wildest imaginings. (99)

Our self love, through the love of God, gives us the strength to move into another level of compassion —- compassion towards others.

COMPASSION TOWARDS OTHERS

Compassion is also developed through our love of others, our compassion not only towards other human beings, but also toward other living entities. The Dalai Lama reveals the most important of the Buddhist principles: "(1) adopting a world view that perceives the interdependent nature of phenomena, that is, the dependently originated nature of all things and events, and (2) based on that, leading a non-violent and non-harming way of life" (*Tibetan* 16).

"First, do no harm" must be the word in our vocabulary of compassion. This incorporates the compassion towards the self and the compassion towards all living things — the plants, animals, humans, Earth, and the cosmos. Compassion comes with a very old but unused vocabulary. It is the language of the soul, a language that has died out in today's world. How infrequently this language is taught in our religious, educational, and political systems; how infrequently it is taught in our family systems. We need to begin teaching and modeling compassion through language, whatever its art form, because language is universal whether it is of dance, music, art, or spoken form. We begin by teaching this language to others, beginning with our children, and to educate ourselves and others about the interrelationship of all of nature and the sacredness of this connection. Celebrating a reverence for each and every species on this planet; teaching respect and awe for the diversity of life. A respect for the plants and animals and how they bless, nurture, and sustain us. An acceptance for the most annoying insect, to that of the silliness of a chipmunk, and to the awe of the majesty of an eagle, we bless and embrace creation. All of God's creatures are divinely blessed.

Although our first order is to do no harm, we understand that living results in death and that in order to live, we often cause suffering. In order to survive, we eat the plants, the grains, and the fruits and vegetables. The nourishment we receive must be blessed. The animals that we use for our survival need to be revered for their gifts of food and material uses. And we only use what we must for our survival — that is the reverence of life.

We need also to embrace our relationships with humanity. We become our best selves in relationship to others. And we teach and model our compassionate selves.

Not only do we grow through our relationships with others, we also help in the development and healing of others. For this life process is one of loving each other, of working to relieve the suffering of others, and of embracing and celebrating the beauty and grace of everyone and of life itself.

I see so much compassion demonstrated on the psychiatric ward where I work, not only from staff, but from patient to patient. One day I brought in a friend's dog for pet therapy. Pet therapy is an incredibly healing process and this was Toby's first time on the unit and he responded beautifully. Toby is a yorkiepoo and at the time, he weighted three pounds (he's now at his fighting weight of five pounds!). We had a full unit of patients that day and ten individuals were in the therapy group that I facilitated. This was a group of mostly depressed and suicidal people and there was a pall hanging over the group. When Toby entered the session, the entire mood of the group changed as the clients responded with delight and joy towards this little dog. They passed him around the circle so that everyone had a chance to hold and play with him. At the end of the circle, one troubled young man who had been making a lot of progress in treatment, looked at a young woman who was still severely depressed and stated, "I think you need to have Toby for the rest of the group because you're still so depressed." The entire group agreed and Toby was hers until the group session ended. This was the simple connection of one person to another, given in compassion and in love. It was also the simple compassion of a creature of the world giving back to the universe.

A compassionate world is also a world in which diversity is celebrated. Diversity of each and every being with all our differences in race, color, nationality, sex, sexual orientation, religious preference, social and economic status, abilities, and all other differences which make us uniquely our own. Diversity that is accepted, embraced, and celebrated. Acceptance is about loving, caring, and compassion; it is about opening our hearts to the divinity within one another and honoring this divinity.

We accept and embrace each and every being. Yet acceptance does not mean inaction. Acceptance is of what is and what could be. What could be is justice placed into action. Living is a process of expansion, of going beyond; we need not be satisfied with complacency. So while we accept each other and life on life's terms, we continue to work to expand our level of acceptance through the healing of ourselves and in the spurring on of others to expand their levels of compassion.

This compassion for others takes place not only on an individual level, but also on a collective level. Collectively for groups of people, for communities, nations, and for the world and the entire human family as well as collectively for the universal soul. Humans need to let go of the narcissistic pride which separates one individual from another, one community from another, one nation from another. Instead, a focus must be placed on embracing the commonalities of being a human on this planet. Letting go of the pride that results in the denigration, hatred, and destruction of others; letting go of the pride which results in separation and alienation. Our focus then becomes one of interdependence with all persons, communities, and nations in order for us to continue as a species, a species that was created to embrace the joy of existence. Because if we do not work together, we may all die together in a cosmic self-regenerative system that can, and will, survive without the destructiveness of humanity.

We need to embrace cooperation and compassion in order not to destroy ourselves and the planet through war, nuclear annihilation, environmental holocaust, or an economic and political climate of competition and overabundance. And this interdependence of compassion must also embrace the Earth and the cosmos, for the universe sustains all of life.

LOVE OF THE EARTH AND COSMOS

Our compassionate self is one that embraces Mother Earth as well as the cosmos and Earth's relationship to the cosmos. We understand that our interconnectedness extends beyond our humanity to all of divinity. We are grounded to the Earth through our root chakra, the chakra which connects to all of life, all of existence. Gaia herself is a living, breathing, expanding force-field of energetic connections that enable her to sustain herself through birth and rebirth. The Earth is also divinely connected to the cosmos; the cosmos is an ever-expanding organism that continues to create in its evolutionary process. This universe is a harmonious system which, out of what seems to be chaos, births creative forces resulting in a dynamic order of existence.

In our previous discussions, we have talked about the need of loving all of creation; we embrace nature, we revere her dignity, power, and grace. We honor her by understanding her relationship with all that she has birthed, for all of existence has life. There is an underlying order in this beauty of nature that maintains life in an incredible pattern of coexistence, because:

> For us humans, to attain that fullness of life, we need not only a God to believe in, but we also need the plants of the earth, the fishes of the sea and the many biochemical processes that fertilise creation with beauty and nourishment; destroy any one aspect and human survival becomes precarious, in fact threatened with extinction. (O'Murchu' 18)

But what have we been doing to this planet, this Earth that has a soul of its own, a soul that relates and interrelates to the soul of the individual? We have been destroying her and she weeps the tears of creation at this destruction. The destruction of the oceans, rain forests, ozone layer, land and ecosystems; the annihilation of thousands upon thousands of plant and animal species; the poisoning of our minds, bodies, and souls as well as the poisoning of the universal mind, body, and soul — we do destroy. And while Gaia herself creates and destroys, she has the capacity to re-create. Humanity's destruction of her, however, does not result in this creative process of rebirth, only in death.

Besides the Earth, how are we destroying the universe? Already mentioned is the poisoning of the universal soul — the destruction of the underlying spirit of creation. And we are also impacting the other planets, stars, and galaxies by sending all types of pollution into the cosmic atmosphere as well as by destroying one of its sacred planets. We are destroying the interdependency of all existence in a narcissistic exercise of believing that the Earth is solely for our use instead of soul-ly for all of creation.

We need to embrace the universe and the soul of the world –- embrace it through our heart of divinity as expressed in our universal story. The only hope for the cosmos is this spiritual awakening. What would this entail? It would entail a return to our roots, to the underlying awe, passion, and compassion that birthed us. Returning to the reverence of Earth and the cosmos by loving and embracing nature; by honoring her divinity; by praising, blessing, and worshipping her. How can one not embrace the numinousity of life? To touch the entire universe through love and compassion. To honor the sacredness of the Sun, stars and Moon by passionate celebration. To vow to honor Gaia by first, doing no harm, and then going beyond that basic principle into love. Connecting totally by giving up oneself to dive into the higher existence of the world soul, knowing that by connecting through our heart, third eye and crown chakras, we are totally united in body, mind, and spirit. For our heart chakra is about compassion, our third eye chakra about insight and intuition, and our crown chakra about our connection to the Divine, the Source of highest existence, our spiritual core. By understanding and relating to the divinity within ourselves, we can connect to the divinity of the universe.

UNION WITH THE BELOVED

The opening to union with the Beloved is the ultimate compassionate act. To love, embrace, trust, and let go into the Divine is to fulfill the destiny of our humanity. We are birthed in compassion and into compassion through God; we return to our sacred depths through this union with the Beloved. In this union, we internalize our understanding of the oneness of life; it is a nonnegotiable fact that resonates within our souls. This connection to the Source requires an expansion of our souls — an expansion that is opened by God, to God. For to open our souls is to touch the Holy in his entirety. To transform from our humanness (our heart) into our divinity, to embrace both the immanent and transcendent nature of life, is why we are here. This is the mystery of our mystical journey.

To love with a passion that is beyond human, to love with a passion that is our birthright, is about a compassionate relationship with the Creator. In our connection with Goddess, we love, honor, praise and bless all that she has birthed and will continue to birth. And in our understanding of this compassion, we recognize that the Source experiences all of what we experience — love, compassion, awe, suffering, pain, joy — on yet a higher plane of existence. So how do we give back love and compassion to God? Matthew Fox indicates we do this by healing others; "To relieve another's pain is to relieve one's own, and to relieve the pain of God, who shares in all the pain of the universe" (288). And we also give back by celebrating our very existence and rejoicing into the depths of our hearts and souls.

When humanity, both on individual and collective levels, works and plays together with the presence and power of the universe, healing results. Our compassionate Mother births and rebirths, uniting us all in a cosmic whirlwind of healing energy that transforms on each and every level from the underlying compassion of the universe, to the love of self, to the compassion for others as well as for the Earth and cosmos, and finally, to the union with the Beloved. This is the mandala of compassion.

Chapter Eleven

LIVING LIFE AS CREATION AND CREATIVITY

The Cosmic Christ Speaks on Creativity

"Give birth to yourself — your lifestyles, your relationships, your learning, your sexuality, your joys, your healing, your work — and build up in one another this same courage to create. Enter the great power of the universe, a power of constant generativity and do not be afraid. For I am with you always when you are creating. I, too, am a Creator, sometimes called *the* Creator. But in fact I ask you to be my companions, to share the birthing of images with me, to be my co-creators. Do not bore me by refusing. Do not scandalize me by saying 'I can't.' Do not oppress Mother Earth and her future by refusing to create and re-create. Come, play with me. Let us create together."

Matthew Fox (211)

As we expand ourselves into furthering our connection with God, we come to utilize the creative gifts bestowed by her, the ultimate birther of all realities. This vast power of creativity began even before the birth of the cosmos, erupted with a Big Bang (although it came out of silence), and continues in the process of birth/death/rebirth in each and every creative endeavor. Creativity is our ability to give back to the cosmos as it has given to us. Creativity generates new realities for all of life and tapping into our innate source of creation is a process that allows all beings to expand into their universal oneness. All sentient beings are creative; to evolve over millions of years is the most incredible account of creativity that has ever been gifted. As human beings provided with the awesome ability to use imagination, we are the ones who have been entrusted to co-create with God. And this is the key — for our creativity can be of goodness or of evil and we must choose how to utilize this gift. For creativity is so powerful, so intense, so much an innate sense within us, that we must express it in some manner.

In exploring creativity, we need to understand its connection to the underlying compassion of the universe. For compassion is the ultimate creative act, allowing the universe and all within it to birth and rebirth. The cosmos has expanded and contracted throughout time in an incredible genesis of life-giving energy. What is compassion and what is creativity besides energy? The Earth, seas, Sun, Moon, stars, planets, mountains, valleys, and sentient and non-sentient life forms all pulsate with the creative hands of the All. She continues to be impregnated, births new realities, allows for destruction and death, and rebirths in this fecund universe. All of life needs to give thanks for the beauty and the immense desire that is exploding within and without. How could we not be grateful for this pulsating, sensual, compassionate universe that reverberates within our very pores? Work, play, art, relationships, ceremony — all of life — is a sensation to be experienced in the fullest, richest connection we can have with the Beloved.

Our creativity takes us to the depths of the soul; in fact, creativity is the being of the soul placed into action. To create is to reach into the past, the present, and eternity in order to birth our own divinity. To deny creativity is to neglect the soul and dishonor the spirit. We are born to create; we have been given imagination and insight in order to co-create with Beloved. This is our God-given destiny — create we must! For creativity *is*. It doesn't need to be made into a product, marketed and sold — it just *is*. This process of creation is the ends to the mean, not the means to an end. In and of itself it is art, a state of being conducted by doing for God.

Yet so often we fear creativity. Fearful of what we find within, fearful of the power of our passion, fearful of what is being called forth, fearful of our own divinity. For creativity is of power, passion, reverence; to open to its very depths is to open to the universe in all her genesis. Our creativity taps into the wisdom and talents of all the ages and of all the ancestors in order to unleash its power of the spirit within and without. And this powerful energy can be of lightness or of darkness; only we can choose how to harness and release it.

These fears of creativity are not trivial ones. Once the decision is made to flow into the creative process, life becomes a changing event. For how difficult it is to make the commitment and to take the responsibility to be creative. Life may never be the same as it will now be viewed through the eyes and the hands of the Beloved. For if I place my life and my creation into these hands of the Divine, the beauty and the power of the creation becomes overwhelming, becomes other-worldly. While the creation will be of me, it will also be beyond me. Am I willing to tap into this power or am I fearful of the results?

What do I do with you,

these hands of mine?

How do I heal,

these hands of mine?

Do I touch, caress,

kiss you through these

gifts of the Goddess,

Or do I set you free to

work your own miracles?

Hands not of my own,

hands of eternity,

of touching and being touched.

Not mine — ours.

This creativity is of passion, the passion of the individual and the passion of Yahweh. Unfortunately, for many of us, passion is also terrifying. We have so often been punished for our passions, for our exuberance, for our joy — be it through the church, our educational institutions, or our families. So when passion starts to bubble within us, we may try to stifle it. Passion is so self-revealing, and this too, is a scary proposition. How we must fear allowing others to connect with our passion through our creativity. Are we really ready to let others see our vulnerable selves, our authentic selves, our passionate selves? For this is the outcome of creativity — we are touched in our passions and touch others with our passions. How revealing, how open, how honest!

And because creativity can be of darkness or of lightness, other fears may confine us. Because if I fully open to the divinity of the goodness of creativity, I also open into the realm of darkness. Remember that life is a dialectic and darkness and lightness envelop one another. So am I strong enough to open to all levels, or do I fear what I may find? Yet darkness can reveal so much in its creativity if it is explored through the light energy of the Beloved. But therein lies the question; can I go into the darkness without becoming corrupted by it? We must remember that Hitler was creative, extremely creative, but that was the creative act of evil. Are we fearful of our own capacity for such evil creativity?

What else do we fear? Perhaps we fear the suffering, the pain, the sorrow that is the result of, as well as results in, the creations we inspire. Because creativity is not just about addition; it is about subtraction. It is about delving into the depths of our soul as well as the heights of our spirit. And sinking into darkness and nothingness can be terrifying. Will we come out of the pain and the sorrow? Will the tears ever end? Will the emptiness and aloneness be filled? Yet in these depths we find our ultimate connection with Goddess — even when she feels absent. In these depths we reach the roots of our being and here we can tap into the wisdom and the oneness of all of creation. Here we find our true compassion; here we find our passion for living and for dying. This then, can lead us into unknown realms of the creative energy of the Divine.

In our creations, we must let go of our fears and delve into faith. For if the Divine has birthed this incredible universe, if he has created life as we experience it today, how can we not let go and let be in our own creativity? We need to trust that we are creator and created — that we have been birthed by the Essence who continues in his joy of the ongoing genesis of the Earth and cosmos.

So who is this artist? It is you and me, for the artist is creativity manifested in each and every person. This is artist as lover — a lover of what has, is, and will be generated through creative expression. A lover of nature, a lover of people, a lover of the cosmos in her total fecundity. A true artist is not one who destroys out of evil, but who births out of love. And while art can be destroyed in the process of creation, this destruction is about subtraction, not of harm. For the true artist is about creating out of joy, beauty, expansiveness, healing, fulfillment, pain, passion, wonder, awe, anger, sorrow, and compassion. And while this art may involve destruction, change, and subtraction, the guiding principle for if it is authentic, holistic art is, does it heal? Does it heal the artist and the receiver of the art? It may disturb and it may cause pain, but these can be of healing as much as joy and wonder. If you have seen the work of Robert Mapplethorpe, his erotic photography portraits, you may be jarred by the intensity of the feelings that arise within you. It may even disturb you, but there is still meaning in such work. Yet others who have been creative have been creative to simply destroy. Herein lies the answer to the difference between goodness and evil in the realm of creativity, for authentic creativity must be of passion and compassion, not of hate and evil.

I conducted a women's spirituality group based on an earlier version of this book. One of the things some of the women struggled with was seeing that they were creative beings. Often, we only see creativity as art or music, not recognizing that our daily duties, as well as our hobbies and leisure activities, are creative. We explored their roles as partners and as parents, their cooking and gardening, their roles on Boards of Directors, their work (both volunteer and employment), their involvement in church activities, their crafts such as jewelry making, their participation in exercise and sports, and their time in silence and in compassion –- all creative activities. By the end of group, they were able to celebrate themselves for the artists they were.

And where do we create? We create in our play and in our work, in our relationships, in ceremonies, in leisure and in our professions, in our homes and in nature, on the Earth and in the sky, in the seas and on the land, by ourselves and with others. For every act is an act of positive creativity if it is of love, passion, and compassion. Every act. How often we hear people say, "I'm not creative." This cannot be true for each and every one of us has been birthed to be co-creators with the All. This is our purpose, to create, and when we deny ourselves this capacity, we deny Goddess her joy in creating with us.

Work, art, play, relationships and ceremony — are we truly involved in these activities to the level of creation, or do we merely go about our days with minimal investment in our lives, with mind-and-body numbing rote awareness? Do we live life consciously or unconsciously? Let us explore these creative endeavors.

WORK

Work is a calling that tells us we need to do such creativity in order to fully birth ourselves. How do we heed this call? Is our work truly a vocation or is it something we do solely because we must do it? For true work is creative, a calling forth from the depths of our souls, a release of the spirit to fly in its grandeur. Work that is prophetic is a calling by God, a calling to utilize our imagination, a calling to expand ourselves to the utmost possibility. Creative work makes our hearts soar; it is about healing. For some work may appear creative, but is not healing; for example, building warplanes, utilizing unethical business practices for financial gain, developing biochemical warfare.

Work is of co-creation — it is enchanting, mystical, and it is placing this mysticism into the prophetic through action. If it is true work, it is a spiritual experience; it is the essence of our being. For creative works of *doing* come out of the creativity of *being*; the mystical to the prophetic. We find grace in our work; we find blessing in our work; we find healing in our work.

When we discuss work as a vocation, we need also to explore another type of work which is the inner work of the soul, for if we do not do our inner work, there will be no authentic outer work. Psychospiritual therapist Jacquelyn Small tells us that, "Psychological work designed to build healthy ego skills is very good work, but without its spiritual counterpart, it will only take you so far. It still leaves us feeling that something is missing until we learn to meet our soul's higher needs as well." (12)

This inner work is about healing our soul and our spirit in order to become our highest selves. This inner work is about getting to the roots of our pain, our grief, our emptiness, and our abandonments. It is about letting go of that false ego, the ego that is narcissistically-based, self-centered, and un-wholly (unholy), and merging into the authentic ego self that is heartfelt and compassion-based. Our inner work may be of a psychological examination of self and psyche and/or of the mystical. Psychological work through counseling including spirituality needs, inner exploration, and self-help groups; mystical work of prayer, meditation, mindfulness, silence and solitude, connecting with nature, and all other practices which allow one to go deeper into one's soul. For out of this inner work comes creativity, healing, and transformation. This inner work is not the narcissistic examination of the self for the sole purpose of feeling better (although this is often the beginning and is healing in its own right), but for the purpose of expanding the self in order to help expand others and to transform the soul of the universe.

Therapy is a form of inner work and utilizing the creative arts is a valuable form of expressive therapy. I worked with a woman who was a survivor of sexual abuse that was perpetrated by her father when she was ages four through eight. Because she did not have the ability to use words to describe this abuse (it was just too painful and she would often regress to these ages), we used art as her form of expression. Her paintings revealed the extent of the horror and terror she felt -- paintings of the abuse and her perpetrator and paintings of her inner torture. Dark, angry pictures mostly done in black and red; childlike drawings of her father created in black and gray with daggers coming out of him and with a picture of a huge penis. In using these creative inner and outer works, she was able to begin her grief process and transform her sorrow.

Yet too often in counseling and in New Age spirituality, the work done is superficial and ego-based in order to feel good. Yet we need to do this ego work to get to our authentic self. In order to let go of the ego, we must have a strong ego to begin with. Often, however, people stop this inner work once they gain their stated purpose of feeling better. What a waste — for to truly heal, we must get to the depths of our existence, we must expand through the pain and sorrow into transformation personally and globally. Inner work is a both/and proposition of being and doing for God; it does not stop at merely feeling good. This type of feeling good is usually transitory. Without the healing at depth, any experience can jar this sense of well-being. New Age spirituality too often is not grounded in the Beloved; it is based on immature, feel-good practices and when someone is traumatized, there is no core, no depth of understanding or connection to All That Is. Without the depth of the inner work, there will be no prophetic outer work.

ART

Art is another area of creative action. Art is any creative endeavor that expands us and those around us; the artist is the bearer of such creation. God, the ultimate artist, delights in this co-creation. And what is such art? It is painting, drawing, prose and poetry, creative cooking, lovemaking, raising a child, working, playing, dancing, singing, acting, mountain climbing, sports, relationships, gardening, ceremony. Whatever the art form, it must expand and heal. Authentic art is art with a joy, a passion, a healing. Art is that which touches us intellectually, emotionally, physically, and spiritually. True art inspires us because it is of the Divine in all of its glory. Explore the work of Rembrandt, listen to the passion of the blues, feel the contours of a sculpture — these are the works of masterful teachers who teach us that art helps us to transform into a higher level of self.

A friend of mine took up painting. She had never been involved in the creative arts before, but felt she needed a release from the stress of her job. This woman was a therapist and most of her work involved working with traumatized women, primarily sexual abuse survivors. She talked about the release she felt whenever she sat down to paint. Using oil as her medium of choice, she loved to paint landscapes as nature was also a connection for her. The smell of the paint, the cleanliness of a fresh canvas, the fun of mixing the colors enticed her. She would describe how she would go to another plane of existence, a place that was above the horrors of life, a place that offered her the ability to nurture herself and connect to the Universe. Was she ever going to sell her paintings? No, but that wasn't the purpose. Healing was the purpose.

Let me paint

the Northern Lights,

Not with the brush

of the artist,

But with the hands

of the Divine.

Intellectually, art is the teacher of beauty, of creation, of a higher level of being. It causes us to wade into the deep thought, the thought that created this world. Intellectually, art is viewed with the consciousness of the self, the Divine, and the consciousness of the cosmos. All art comes from thought; all art begins with the creative word of God.

Emotionally, art teaches us to feel, touch, see, hear, taste, visualize, inhale, exhale, imbibe, and devour beauty and truth. What can have a deeper feeling, more emotion, and more passion than art? If we cannot relate to art, whatever its form, we are void of human emotions in a world which is filled with the gorgeous complexion of creation.

Art may also teach us physically for authentic art reaches into our hearts and our inner being. Who hasn't had goose bumps when involved in creation, whether by storytelling, watching an Olympian win a gold medal, or touching a creation of the artist? Who hasn't been kicked in the stomach by art with a vital message, a gut reaction that disturbs? Who hasn't felt the opening of the heart, often experienced as intense pain around the heart, when overwhelmed with the pain of inner creativity? Who hasn't shed a tear when watching a child's first theatrical performance or when completing a beautiful poem? We are so physically touched by this glory of imagination, this glory of pleasure, this connection of human meeting divine.

And finally, we recognize that art delves into our spiritual connection to the Oneness. The muses fill us with mystery in their delight of art. Art is both immanent and transcendent. It connects us to the sense of awe, the underlying passion and compassion of the universe, and to the joy, wonder, and delight that is God. Authentic art deepens us. This is the artist who is touched and nourished by creation and who then translates this into nourishment for all. To be able to create as an artist is one of our tasks. The intensity, the wellspring of the birth of art is an ecstasy of humankind.

Here are the words of this artist as written in 2003.

I awaken to the silent whispers which reveal a plan that is reflective of both inner and outer work — write. Write, I'm told as I drift into sleep; write I'm told upon awakening; write when thoughts go flying through my head; write when I pick up a pen and note pad. But what do I write? It doesn't matter; it will be given. So I write. Poetry. Book chapters. Divine revelations. Divine revelations — how grandiose is that thinking? But they're there; words of such wisdom that they obviously don't come from this human form. They come of their own accord, without warning, without planning, without effort; poetry and prose that sing of their own soul. So I honor them by the only way I know how, by using my human self to reveal the divine self. These whispers that come in silence, through the opening of the heart to the core of the soul, come as a gift of God. And like all gifts, unwrapping the present is as delicious a part of the gift as the present itself. Writing is my unwrapping.

In the writing is the joy, creativity and passion that underlies all of existence — the compassion of the Creator and the created. A delight and awe in all that has been provided, the joy and the sorrow, the lightness and darkness, the emptiness and the fullness, a delight in the dialectic of life. Writing that is a sensual process which is Source-based and divinely provided.

"Source-based and divinely provided"; this is the true meaning of art and artist. This is our blessing of inspiration. This is blessing.

PLAY

An often overlooked creative endeavor is that of play and leisure. We have been placed on this Earth by a Creator who has a sense of humor. We only have to watch her creations in action — the chimpanzees, chipmunks, cats and dogs, and babies of all creatures — to understand that creativity is based upon play. What fun, what delight we creatures of God provide the universe. In this joy, all of creation lets go and imbibes in play, in the at-the-moment frivolity of life. God must be so pleased in what she has birthed on land and stream; such imagination!

And as the Beloved demonstrates such a sense of humor, so must his co-creators. Humor, fun, play, and leisure are as much a human right as the right of the Divine. For to be truly alive, we must celebrate, enjoy, and experience pleasure and ecstasy. We are delighted and delightful creations who must revel in our own passions and creativity.

For what is play but a celebration of the blessings of this life. A celebration of life and living. In our celebration we understand that we have been created in grace and we bless the Beloved as she has blessed us. To have fun is to say "thank you" — thank you for birthing me into this lifetime, thank you for such gifts. To never celebrate, to remain stoic, to subvert our passions is to dishonor the Essence.

In our play, we learn. We develop necessary life skills such as how to relate to others. We expand our physical prowess, develop our intellect, and feel our emotions. We also learn about what pleases us, what pleasure is, and how fun is a joy in life. This then, is a spiritual process as play teaches us that life is meant to be fully experienced in delight, even in the midst of difficulties. The entire universe expands out of this play which is so very healing. In Diane Ackerman's book, *Deep Play*, we learn that:

> Every element of the human saga requires play. We evolved
> through play. Our culture thrives on play. Courtship includes
> high theater, rituals, and ceremonies of play. Ideas are playful
> reverberations of the mind. Language is a playing with words
> until they can impersonate physical objects and abstract ideas.
> (3-4)

Yet Ackerman further distinguishes between play and deep play for "deep play always involves the sacred and holy, sometimes hidden in the most unlikely or humble places [. . .]" (13). In this deep play, we touch into the realm of the mystical, for such play is transcendent. In our ecstasy of play, we reach a higher level of being, a deeper connection to self and to divinity. We hear athletes discuss reaching "the zone," that mystical level of play that takes them out of their everyday capabilities into a transcendent state of being beyond themselves with skill levels that are unfathomable. We listen to musicians relating their own "zone," of being in another dimension of time and space when they are performing. We know how intense, loving, and committed sexual experiences are ones of merging with the partner into the essence of the Beloved. These are the gifts of sacred play, deep play.

Such play is a freeing of the spirit, allowing it to rise into another dimension of creativity. Such play is of rapture, intensity, and commitment. It may be spontaneous, it may be planned, but its deepest element is of the sacred sense of being in the world and beyond. It is a harmony within the total existence of life.

One of my most fascinating experiences was conducting a group at a men's and women's chemical dependency treatment facility during Easter. We talked about the significance of spring and rebirth and eggs as fertility and new life. Then they had the assignment of coloring the eggs. While the women immediately began this task and enjoyed this activity, most of the men were hesitant, telling me it was a lame, stupid, and childish assignment. With persuasion, they began to color the eggs. What a transformation! The men became engaged in the process and were laughing and having fun. When I hid the eggs for them outdoors, the men were as excited as the women in searching for the eggs and getting prizes for their finds. A simple creative, child-like activity transformed some of these hardened addicts (many with criminal histories) into the playful souls that they were, but that had been subverted by the addictions.

RELATIONSHIPS

Another important aspect of creativity is that of relationships. Being in a relationship is perhaps our most difficult, and therefore, the most powerful creative act. For how to relate to another human being — to love, honor, respect, commit, trust and let go — is an act of unselfishness and an act of the mystical. This level of intimacy is a creative endeavor, for developing connections to one another and to the Beloved is why we are here. As already discussed, we are here to learn compassion, the ultimate act of creativity.

So what is a creative relationship? It is one that allows us and the other person to be vulnerable, open, intimate, caring, honest, compassionate, understanding, connected, joyful, sad, angry, hurt, and fun-loving. In this relationship, integrity is valued, for what am I if I am not of integrity? These characteristics lead to intimacy, intimacy which "has a mystical quality because through our union with another person we begin to feel a greater oneness with All That Is." And, as Charlotte Kasl continues:

> The river that flows in us flows through all things. Intimacy carries the seeds of transformation because it expands our hearts, allowing us to see life from the big perspective of compassion and understanding. Intimacy brings the music and the words together, allowing us to dissolve into one another while remaining conscious of our separate journeys. (11)

Expanding our hearts is an experience that opens us to a deeper connection to our friends, family, partner, and the Divine. For when we open our hearts, we allow the mystical to enter. Petty concerns, tribulations, hurts, self-righteousness, and judgment disappear as we transform our ego concerns into the realm of the spirit. We experience the sacred in the other person as we open to the mysteries of the heart chakra. We experience the plethora of compassion and love of creation, for love and compassion define our universal existence if we so allow them. Let us do so in our relationships, and we will heal the pain of the Earth and the cosmos and all who reside within.

I have experienced this type of intimacy one time in my life. While there have been relationships that were intimate on physical and emotional levels, only one was spiritually intimate. This level of connection was a merging of our physical, emotional, and spiritual selves that took both of us into the immanent connection as well as a transcendent level of union. I still cannot find the words to adequately express this merging of ourselves into the Beloved, where time and space evolved into eternity. This is the ultimate connection of intimacy.

CEREMONY

Finally, we need to explore ceremonies and rituals as sacred, creative acts. For such ceremonies are about celebration and celebration is about appreciating the creative moments of our lives. To rejoice in our daily blessings of life, health, abundance, joy and beauty; to rejoice in God/Goddess is about grace and goodness. Celebration, ritual, and ceremony are ways to give back to the Creator, to bless as we have been blessed. For we have come upon this Earth for a purpose — to learn to connect more intimately with one another and with the Beloved. How could we not celebrate our being? Ceremonies and rituals to connect to nature, celebrations of birth and rituals of death, rites of passage into adolescence and into the wisdom of the Crone, into commitment with another human being, spiritual and religious practices — all help us to connect to the universe and to the mystery of living. These mystical celebrations touch us to our core as the poetry of healing, the dance of sensations, the awe of blessing and being blessed. Celebration is a renaissance of spirit in which the human meets divine.

How do we know when we're in the sacredness of creativity? We feel it in our bones and in our heart. Time stands still in our creativity as art is of the eternal. This is the deep, deep connection to the All — where time stands still. We enter into a higher consciousness, a consciousness of mystical union with the Divine. When we are creating for the sacred, we operate out of passion and compassion. We are in the totality of creation; we are eternity itself. We are enfolded in the wings of cherubim; we become angels ourselves. And we must take flight. For, "The highest nature of all pleasure is that aspect of pleasure which causes you to create Who You Really Are in your experience right here, right now — and to re-create, and re-create, and re-create again Who You Are at the next highest level of magnificence. That is the highest pleasure of God" (Walsch 53). And in our re-creation, we expand into our highest selves by honoring the call for service and justice-making.

Chapter Twelve

THE PROPHETIC CALL:
SERVICE AND JUSTICE-MAKING

Selfless service cannot come out of a denial of a personal motivation and objective. Even though you really care about others and want to help them, your spiritual journey is your own, determined by your unique karma. It is only at the conclusion of the journey that, as Ramakrishna says, you throw into the fire both the thorn (attachments) removed from your foot and the thorn (spiritual practice) you used to remove the other thorn. Only then, when, as Gandhi says, the surrender to God is complete, does true selfless service emerge.

Ram Dass (58)

While we are all wired to become mystics, we must learn to become prophets for prophecy is the action step of mysticism. Remember that mysticism is about the inner journey of the self into the depths of the soul; it is the mystery of the connection of the self to the Absolute. Mysticism is receptivity that is contemplation on a level of stillness, of oneness. It is our calling back to the Beloved -- to the ground of our being through reaching and touching the sky. Our journey into ourselves is the journey into creation; this is the essence of mysticism. For mystery is related to the sacred interconnection of all life as all beings dance to the universal tune of oneness.

Out of this mysticism, the true contemplative flows into prophetic movement. This mystic in action is a person who, grounded in the sacredness of all of life, walks the talk. This is the mystic who recognizes the need to externalize what has been birthed through the process of mysticism. For to truly be a prophet, one has to have internalized the essence of being developed through the connection to the universal All.

Mysticism needs to be balanced with the prophetic and the prophetic must be balanced by mysticism. Why? Because mysticism without prophecy can become a narcissistic endeavor of self-indulgent transcendence and prophecy without mysticism can become a cause without a heart. In our mysticism, we can slip into an ecstasy of self-centeredness because by focusing only on our inner being, be it of joy or of sorrow, we may become focused only in trying to touch the Divine One to the exclusion of touching others. If we are attempting to reach transcendence only for ourselves, we are missing the purpose of this incarnation. To be fully contemplative, we need to go beyond our own interests into the interests of others, the global community, and beyond. This is when the prophetic voice becomes most important.

Yet we must also apply the principles of mysticism to the social action of the prophet. If not, the actions of the prophet may be based on egoism, those based on what "I" believe is necessary for justice making, not what Spirit asks. And who am "I" to make such decisions alone? Through the connection to the oneness of life, we can understand the tenets of heaven and Earth and be guided to seek justice out of love and compassion instead of ego.

We begin to give birth to our prophetic voice by first listening to our soul, entering into the mystery, and then delving into co-creation with God. For creativity is birth and rebirth -- of ourselves, our spirits, and our being with the creative energy of the Beloved. This birth is the prophetic -- our heartfelt connection placed into the artwork of our actions. These actions are the *doing* of and for Goddess which has transformed out of the *being* for Goddess. For being for God and doing for God is our destiny.

This creativity is revealed in so many ways. It is a type of prayer, a focus on gratefulness that expresses itself in the beauty and the joy that is created. It is a type of meditation, for to produce such creativity, the mystical reveals herself in the silence and peace. It is mindful — to let go of everything but the creation. This creativity may come from the silence and emptiness or the expansiveness and joy that are the underlying awe of the universe itself. And out of this outpouring of Spirit, the prophetic voice is given rise. True art is prophetic — it speaks its own truth.

Out of pain and sorrow we learn to become more compassionate beings as we begin to relate to the pain and suffering of others. As we expand into our depths of compassion, we learn that we are here to help transform such pain. We are guided to expand ourselves and to help others expand themselves — to continue to grow into the Divine. This compassion continues to transform into justice making and social action for we begin to realize that when one suffers, all suffer, and if we relieve the suffering of one, it transforms into healing the suffering of all, including the suffering of the universe. This is our social consciousness which is directly connected to the consciousness of the Creator. We do the good works of the Beloved; we co-create with him by working to transform the ills of society. And in working toward such healing, we ourselves are healed. For, "Whether our compassionate action is done alone or in a group, inner exploration remains the complement to external action, and, with time and patience, it can lead to clearer awareness, action with more integrity, and a freer flow of the heart's breath" (Bush, in Dass and Bush 220).

In the work of the prophet, we must explore our potential actions in order to assess whether they are acts of selflessness or acts of selfishness. For harmful deeds have been perpetrated under the misguided beliefs that justice was being served. These acts of service need to come from our spiritual depths for to complete acts without selflessness is to denigrate those who are being helped. In our actions, we need to explore further aspects of the self. Ram Dass outlines a path of action noting that it:

- is in harmony with our values
- uses our particular skills, talents, and personality characteristics
- makes use of our opportunities
- acknowledges our liabilities as well as our assets
- takes into account existing responsibilities
- is honoring the diverse roles we are called upon to fulfill in the moment.

(136)

These actions are placed into motion to serve individuals, communities, the global community, the Earth and cosmos, the Beloved, and the underlying soul of the universe. While all good work is of the prophetic, we will examine three compassionate practices which may include prayer (especially community prayer); the Buddhist practice of tonglen; and justice-making endeavors such as working towards peace, protecting the environment, and helping to heal the social ills of society.

The question recently arose in a discussion during a spirituality group I facilitate regarding how prayer can be beneficial. A group member noted her struggle with those persons who focus only on prayer and not on specific actions of justice making. She indicated it was difficult to see how prayer was enough in these turbulent times. And while I understood this concern — for I too get frustrated when people don't engage in social action — my response was one of wondering where our world would be today if not for the prayers of all those persons — the monks, nuns, the cloistered, the prayer groups and all others who have prayed for centuries for peace and healing. For prayers that are set forth by individuals and by groups for cosmic healing are just as valuable as the direct actions taken by those of us who are involved in more extroverted activities. And as studies show (see especially the work of Larry Dossey), prayer heals. So a prophetic call may be one that is seen as silent but also bursts forth with its power and passion for healing. Prayer, meditation, chanting, and music heal us to our individual core; how could we not believe they heal to the universal core?

As we discuss more individual and introverted justice-making practices, we need to explore the Buddhist practice of tonglen, which is a practice of accepting the pain and suffering of others, grieving it, and blessing it by focusing on healing; this is done in conjunction with breathing. Breathing in pain, and exhaling light, peace, and love. Pema Chodron outlines a four step process for tonglen:

1. Flashing openness
2. Working with the texture, breathing in dark, heavy, and hot and breathing out white, light, and cool
3. Working with relieving a specific, heartfelt instance of suffering
4. Extending that wish to help everyone. (43)

This is a practice that can be conducted individually or in groups. It too, is a practice of justice making, a way to help heal the world through accepting the pain of the universe and transforming it into light energy. This, however, can be a difficult process because to accept the grief of individuals or the grief of the world is to feel to our depths the intense sorrow that exists around and through us. We cannot help but feel the sadness, horror, terror, abandonment, and emptiness that is a reality for so many persons as well as for the Earth and her other sentient inhabitants. We feel the grief of the universal soul which sobs in its pain. We feel the Divine's tears that are wept over the destruction of its species and the planet in man's terrible wake of power, control, and hate.

Whether we practice tonglen or we are persons who naturally experience the sorrow of those around us, we must continue to honor the process of the task to grieve and to help heal this sorrow. Out of sorrow comes the transformation not only for ourselves, but for all other sentient beings. This is the task of justice making.

And finally, we must take social action, to place justice making in the companionship of extroverted practices. To be of service to others is to walk in the steps of Buddha, Mother Theresa, Martin Luther King, Jr., Jesus, Gandhi, Hildegard of Bingen; to walk with all of those prophets who have walked before us and who walk with us today. To walk with the lepers, to hold the hands of those who have AIDS, to feed the starving, to house the homeless, to bath the sick, to fight for funding for the mentally ill and the chemically dependent, to illuminate the eyes of those who have lost sight of compassion, to eradicate racial and sexual injustice, to save the whales and the dolphins, to protest nuclear weapons, to educate the illiterate; these are the actions of the prophets. These are the actions of mystics who embrace compassionate service.

Our prophetic work transforms the global community and the universe through mysticism in action. For if each individual begins to do the necessary inner and outer work, that individual begins to heal. As individuals heal, they develop the capacity to help others to heal. And this healing expands into the global community including the Earth and the cosmos. Through our mysticism, our souls are touched by prayer, meditation, inner contemplation, blessings, gratefulness, opening the heart, in silence and solitude, in emptiness and in fullness, and in our daily experiences. We learn to caress the Divine with a new level of openness, a deeper level of connection. In this manner, we give back to creation as creation has given to us. We are both healer and heal-ee.

In the late 1980s, I was just beginning to explore my spirituality and was beginning to get more involved in GLBT issues. I was especially struggling with how so many churches took a stand of prejudice and discrimination against homosexuals. At this time, I began to see a young man for therapy who was attending a fundamentalist Christian church and who was questioning the church's beliefs and actions with regard to homosexuality. He wanted to stay in the church since he related to much of their doctrine and he enjoyed relationships with many of the parishioners. But when he told me some of their basic tenets and then said they held an intervention for him (to try to get him to stop acting on his homosexuality and to change his sexual orientation), it was all I could do to stop myself from exclaiming my own spiritual and political beliefs, for I wanted him to leave the church and its homophobia. I continued to work with him for many months and I learned so much from him. He decided to stay within the church and he became an influential voice within the church regarding his beliefs of acceptance, love, and compassion towards all people. He served as a role model for others who didn't understand homosexuality and he helped many members overcome their prejudices. He was also a role model for me as he helped me to learn compassion towards people with fundamentalist beliefs (something I still struggle with even 20 years later), and he helped me to understand my own self-righteousness. This was a man who was a mystic and a prophet. I hope he's continued on this path.

For unless these mystical experiences are utilized to bless others, we miss the purpose that was granted by the Creator. We are here to speak the truth, to be the compassionate voice for those who can't speak and for those who suffer. Through our prophetic visions of creativity, we burst forth into the transformation of healing the Earth and her beings, the Earth and her soul, the Earth and her surrounding universe. We are here to go beyond our humanness into the blessings of Beloved. In our compassion and our prophetic work, we reach unity with the Absolute. This is the joy of working together as one — the ecstasy of shared intimacies, shared growth, and shared transformation. We rejoice and celebrate the oneness of life. This is the deepest level of compassion, a relationship to All That Is. Andrew Harvey reminds us that:

> In all the serious mystical traditions, the final aim of the Path is not ecstasy, or revelation, or the possession of amazing powers, or any kind of *purely personal fulfillment*, however inspired or exalted, but to become the humble, supple, selfless, and tireless instrument of God and servant of divine love. (271)

Part Five:

Union with the Beloved

Finally, in Section Five, we examine union with the Beloved through a discussion of the human/divine connection — where immanence meets transcendence — and how we must utilize this union to transform creation. Our journeys begin and end in such divine union.

Chapter Thirteen

WHERE ALL OUR JOURNEYS END

No End

The goal of travelers is to reach their destination; what could be the destination or end to those who have attained Union, in which there can never be any separation?

They travel on and on, from bliss to finer bliss, from knowledge to ignorance to wilder knowledge, from peace to ever-deepening and expanding peace.

A vain fool came to me and said: "I have attained Union! My Journey is over!" I said: "Never blaspheme like that again! If you had attained union, your real journey would just be beginning!" But why throw pearls on a dung-heap?

The journey to Him ends with the revelation of His Glory; the journey *in* Glory can never end, for Glory is boundless and its wonders are infinite.

And the Law is: No ripe grape ever again becomes unripe; no mature fruit ever again becomes green.

Rumi (Harvey, *Light* 228)

In our search for the Beloved, we discover a paradox — our journeys never end, for our destiny is endless. Life is a dialectic. Our travels into the Divine may feel like the final destination, and in one sense, the journey has ended in such union, but in another sense, the journey has just begun into the expansiveness of the universal oneness of our being.

Mystics speak of the divine union with Goddess, of the totality of the connection, the bliss of oneness, the ecstasy of being and non-being. And what a magical sensation this is! To feel the completeness of the universe, to understand the truths of existence, to revel in the peace and joy which surpasses all understanding, is the most incredible experience in this human form. For union is that which is of immanence and beyond immanence, that which is of the transcendent nature which is deeply embedded in each and every soul. How beautiful is the experience, how enchanting is the moment. For we are all meant to experience union; to completely encompass the light and love of God. It is the total consummation of being a divine human or a human divine. It is faith and beyond faith. It is God and beyond God. It is the totality of love.

Have you felt such perfect love? Have you felt such merging into the Beloved? Through the eyes of a loved one, in prayer or meditation, sacred sex, dancing, painting, walking along a deserted beach, singing, wind surfing, watching a child — have you felt it? That rapture of total union, that ecstasy of completeness, that compassion and love that bathes over you like a fresh mountain stream. It may have been for a minute, an hour, a day, an eternity — but it is there.

We are all children of the Beloved who are wired to such divine oneness. Maybe we've only felt a slight tug of such union, an instant of this magical bliss. Or maybe we live in such oneness daily, to the mystical level of such divinized beings such as Rumi and Shams, Hildegard of Bingen, Christ, Mohammed, Buddha, Julian of Norwich. We are all mystics who can achieve all levels of union — not better, but different levels of union, as we all have paths to follow in our journeys of everyday life.

We are all mystics on this path as we have all been graced with the divinity that is our birthright. We may not as yet have tapped into such a level of transcendence, but it is awaiting us all. This essence of merging may come with another human being or it may be an individual process; whatever its course, it is a level of completeness that is life-defining.

The Christian mystics have long revered three stages of mysticism — purgation, illumination, and union. Andrew Harvey, in *Son of Man*, expands upon these paths to include a fourth state, birthing. Purgation is the awakening stage, where God's presence becomes a reality and a spiritual discipline is begun. In this stage, we go through experiences of developing into a new way of living. Suffering occurs at this stage and is infused with divine love.

Stage 2, Illumination, relates to the empowered nature of the person who experiences greater gifts of creativity, whatever that creativity may be. One becomes highly intuitional, receives greater awareness and clarity, and goes through the experience of the Dark Night. This becomes an act of complete surrender.

Stage 3, Union, is the Sacred Marriage between human and divine; for, "All the powers of body, mind, heart, and soul are united in a fire of human divine love; the universe is experienced as a constant dance of supreme consciousness" (Harvey, *Son* 117). This is the stage of merging. This is the Oneness of the All, the Oneness of the Universe, the totality of the Union. This is the Alpha and the Omega.

And while we may believe that our journeys end here, for union with the Divine is an incredible experience of bliss, rapture, joy and transcendence, Harvey relates that there is a Stage 4, that of Birthing. He states, "Union is, in fact, the beginning of another unbounded and endless journey into ever-higher and ever-greater divine being" (*Son* 123). This is the stage of activism and justice-making; this is the stage where divinized human beings expand beyond the self into the healing of the universe and the Universal Oneness. This is the regeneration of life and of love transformed by action.

So our search for the Beloved takes place in each and every thing we do and each and everything we be. We recognize that there is no beginning and no end, for in all our journeys, the end of the journey is the beginning. Our search takes us back to ourselves; our search finds Beloved within us always. This is the path of the mandala that was previously discussed, which reverberates in and around us and that teaches us the truth that the path of awakening is endlessly creative. There is always a higher level of divinity that awaits us. In our union, we taste that oneness of life which is love, simply love. In our union, we not only are love, we *be* love. And we are not meant to only bask in such bliss, but to rejoice and celebrate such being with all others.

What is such union? I found it in the merging with my beloved where we were enveloped in Oneness. This was so intense, so connected and so loving, that I felt myself totally immersed into the soul of the universe. This union lasted for hours and I was able to bask in seeing creation as the totality of our purpose for being on Earth. I knew at that moment that my life was forever changed, as my ego was annihilated into the merging of All That Is (if only for a few hours).

Oh where is my Beloved

today, today,

Oh where is my Beloved today?

Is she hiding under this rock

or behind this tree?

Perhaps she's nestled deep within the sea

or in the ashes of a burned out forest.

Does she only exist in a church, synagogue

or mosque?

Maybe she's playing hide-and-seek

and torturing me with her pleasure.

Perhaps she doesn't exist for someone

like me — black, white, agnostic, fat, skinny, pagan,

short, tall, happy, sad, gay, straight, rich, poor, atheist.

Oh where is my Beloved

today, today,

Oh where is my Beloved today?

She is here, everywhere, in the depths of our souls and the heights of the cosmos where our spirits run free. She is in every face, every action, every sentient and non-sentient being — in the rocks, the stars, the birds and the animals, the land and the sea. She is in every blessing and every trauma. For within every heart, God resides. As we have explored in each chapter, God is who we are. In our senses and sensuality, in our sexuality, our joy and sorrow, in darkness and in light, in nature, and in solitude and silence, Goddess is. Through prayerful living, in compassion and creativity, in mysticism and prophecy, in service and justice-making, in union and in passion, the Beloved is always here. Ever present, ever loving, ever compassionate. Our duty is to come home to such divinity; this is the blessing of mankind. As Wiccan practitioner Starhawk relates:

> The Goddess awakens in infinite forms and a thousand disguises. She is found where She is least expected, appears out of nowhere and everywhere to illumine the open heart. She is singing, crying, moaning, wailing, shrieking, crooning to us: to be awake, to commit ourselves to life, to be a lover in the world and of the world, to join our voices in the single song of constant change and creation. For Her law is love unto all beings, and She is the cup of the drink of life. (229)

Let us all drink of this cup.

Works Cited: Chapter One

Harvey, Andrew. *The Return of the Mother*. Berkeley: Frog, 1995.

Helminski, Kabir. *Living Presence: A Sufi Way to Mindfulness and the Essential Self*. New York: Tarcher, 1992.

Underhill, Evelyn. *Mysticism: The Nature and Development of Spiritual Consciousness*. Chatham, NY: Oneworld, 1993.

Walsch, Neale Donald. *Conversations with God: An Uncommon Dialogue — Book 1*. Charlottesville, VA: Hampton Roads, 1995.

Works Cited: Chapter Two

Barks, Coleman, Trans. "The Morning Wind." *The Essential Rumi.* New York: HarperSanFrancisco, 1995.

Doyle, Brendan. "I Understood." *Meditations with Julian of Norwich.* Santa Fe: Bear, 1983.

Myss, Caroline. *Anatomy of the Spirit: The Seven Stages of Power and Healing.* New York: Three Rivers, 1996.

Nhat Hanh, Thich. *Going Home: Jesus and Buddha as Brothers.* New York: Riverhead, 1999.

Zukav, Gary. *The Seat of the Soul.* New York: Fireside, 1989.

Works Cited: Chapter Three

Barks, Coleman, Trans. "They Try." *The Essential Rumi.* New York: HarperSanFrancisco, 1995.

———. "Where Everything is Music." *The Essential Rumi.* New York: HarperSanFrancisco, 1995.

Barks, Coleman, Trans. and Michael Green. *The Illuminated Rumi.* New York: Broadway, 1997.

Fox, Matthew. *The Coming of the Cosmic Christ: The Healing of Mother Earth and the Birth of a Global Renaissance.* New York: HarperSanFrancisco, 1988.

Kaufman, Gershen and Lev Raphael. *Coming Out of Shame: Transforming Gay and Lesbian Lives.* New York: Doubleday, 1996.

Moore, Thomas. *The Soul of Sex: Cultivating Life as an Act of Love.* New York: HarperCollins, 1998.

Works Cited: Chapter Four

Chodron, Pema. *The Places That Scare You: A Guide to Fearlessness in Difficult Times.* Boston: Shambhala, 2001.

———. *Start Where You Are: A Guide to Compassionate Living.* Boston: Shambhala, 1994.

Dalai Lama and Howard C. Cutler. *The Art of Happiness: A Handbook for Living.* New York: Riverhead Books, 1998.

Walsch, Neale Donald. *Friendship with God: An Uncommon Dialogue.* New York: G.P. Putnam's Sons, 1999.

Works Cited: Chapter Five

Barks, Coleman, Trans. "The Guest House." *The Essential Rumi.* New York: HarperSanFrancisco, 1995.

Gibran, Kahlil. "And a Woman Spoke." *The Prophet.* New York: Knopf, 1956.

Grof, Christina and Stanislav Grof. *The Stormy Search for the Self: A Guide to Personal Growth through Transformational Crisis.* New York: Tarcher/Putnam, 1990.

Moore, Thomas. *Care of the Soul: A Guide for Cultivating Depth and Sacredness in Everyday Life.* New York: HarperPerennial, 1992.

St. John of the Cross. *The Dark Night of the Soul and The Living Flame of Love.* Comp. Robert Van de Weyer. London: Fount, 1995.

Welwood, John. "Depression as a Loss of Heart: Opening to Healing Through Inner Work." *Sacred Sorrows: Embracing and Transforming Depression.* Eds. John Nelson and Andrea Nelson. New York: Tarcher/Putnam, 1996. 160-167.

Works Cited: Chapter Six

Buber, Martin. *Good and Evil*. Trans. Michael Bullock. New York: Charles Scribner, 1953.

Doyle, Brendan. "We See." *Meditations with Julian of Norwich*. Santa Fe: Bear, 1983.

Keen, Sam. "The Enemy Maker." *Meeting the Shadow: The Hidden Power of the Dark Side of Human Nature*. Eds. Connie Zweig and Jeremiah Abrams. Los Angeles: Jeremy Tarcher, 1991. 197 - 202.

Peck, M. Scott. *People of the Lie: The Hope for Healing Human Evil*. New York: Touchstone, 1983.

Sanford, John. "Dr. Jekyll and Mr. Hyde." *Meeting the Shadow: The Hidden Power of the Dark Side of Human Nature*. Eds. Connie Zweig and Jeremiah Abrams. Los Angeles: Jeremy Tarcher, 1991. 29 - 34.

Storr, Anthony. *The Essential Jung*. Princeton, NJ: Princeton U., 1983.

Zukav, Gary. *The Seat of the Soul*. New York: Fireside, 1989.

Works Cited: Chapter Seven

Christ, Carol P. "Rethinking Theology and Nature." *Weaving the Visions: New Patterns in Feminist Spirituality.* Eds. Judith Plaskow and Carol P. Christ. San Francisco: Harper & Row, 1989. 314 – 325.

Keck, L. Robert. *Sacred Quest: The Evolution and Future of the Human Soul.* West Chester, PA: Chrysalis Books, 2000.

Roberts, Elizabeth and Elias Amidon, Eds. "O Great Spirit." *Earth Prayers from Around the World: 365 Prayers, Poems, and Invocations for Honoring the Earth.* New York: HarperSanFranciso, 1991.

Swimme, Brian and Thomas Berry. *The Universe Story: From the Primordial Flaring Forth to the Ecozoic Era, A Celebration of the Unfolding of the Cosmos.* New York: HarperSanFrancisco, 1992.

Thoreau, Henry David. *Walden, or Life in the Woods.* New York: Signet, 1964.

Uhlein, Gabriele, Ed. "With Nature's Help." *Meditations with Hildegard of Bingen.* Santa Fe: Bear, 1983.

Works Cited: Chapter Eight

Fox, Matthew. *Passion for Creation: The Earth-Honoring Spirituality of Meister Eckhart.* Rochester, VT: Inner Traditions, 1980, 2000.

Harvey, Andrew, trans. and adapted. "To Enjoy This Conversation." *Light Upon Light: Inspirations from Rumi.* Berkeley: North Atlantic, 1996.

Merton, Thomas. *A Search for Solitude: Pursuing the Monk's True Life.* Ed. Lawrence Cunningham. New York: HarperCollins, 1996.

Storr, Anthony. *Solitude: A Return to the Self.* New York: Ballentine, 1988.

Underhill, Evelyn. *Mysticism: The Nature and Development of Spiritual Consciousness.* Chartham, NY: Oneworld, 1993.

Works Cited: Chapter Nine

Dossey, Larry. *Healing Words: The Power of Prayer and the Practice of Medicine*. New York: HarperSanFrancisco, 1993.

Harvey, Andrew, trans. and adapted. "They Continue at Their Prayers." *Light Upon Light: Inspirations from Rumi*. Berkeley: North Atlantic Books, 1996.

Steindl-Rast, David. *Gratefulness, the Heart of Prayer: An Approach to Life in Fullness*. Mahwah, NJ: Paulist Press, 1984.

Works Cited: Chapter Ten

Dalai Lama (Tenzin Gyatso). *The Power of Compassion: A Collection of Lectures by His Holiness the XIV Dalai Lama*. Trans. Geshe Thupten Jinpa. San Francisco: Thorsons, 1981.

———. *The World of Tibetan Buddhism: An Overview of Its Philosophy and Practice*. Trans., ed., and annotated by Geshe Thupten Jinpa. Boston: Wisdom, 1995.

Fox, Matthew. *Original Blessing: A Primer in Creation Spirituality*. Santa Fe: Bear, 1983.

Harvey, Andrew. *Son of Man: The Mystical Path to Christ*. New York: Tarcher/Putnam, 1998.

Kasl, Charlotte. *A Home for the Heart: Creating Intimacy and Community with Loved Ones, Neighbors, and Friends*. New York: HarperCollins, 1997.

O' Murchu', Diarmuid. *Reclaiming Spirituality*. New York: Crossroad, 1999.

Peck, M. Scott. *Further Along the Road Less Traveled: The Unending Journey Toward Spiritual Growth*. New York: Simon & Schuster, 1993.

Swimme, Brian. *The Universe is a Green Dragon: A Cosmic Creation Story*. Sante Fe: Bear, 1984.

Works Cited: Chapter Eleven

Ackerman, Diane. *Deep Play*. New York: Vintage, 2000.

Fox, Matthew. *The Coming of the Cosmic Christ: The Healing of Mother Earth and the Birth of a Global Renaissance*. New York: HarperSan-Francisco, 1988.

Kasl, Charlotte. *A Home for the Heart: Creating Intimacy and Community with Loved Ones, Neighbors, and Friends*. New York: HarperCollins, 1997.

Small, Jacquelyn. *The Sacred Purpose of Being Human: A Healing Journey Through the 12 Principles of Wholeness*. Deerfield Beach, FL: Health Communications, 2005.

Walsch, Neale Donald. *Conversations with God: An Uncommon Dialogue — Book 3*. Charlottesville, VA: Hampton Roads, 1998.

Works Cited: Chapter Twelve

Chodron, Pema. *Start Where You Are: A Guide to Compassionate Living.*
    Boston: Shambhala, 1994.
Dass, Ram and Mirabai Bush. *Compassion in Action: Setting Out on the
    Path of Service.* New York: Bell Tower, 1992.
Harvey, Andrew. *The Direct Path: Creating a Journey to the Divine Using
    the World's Mystical Traditions.* New York: Broadway, 2000.

Works Cited: Chapter Thirteen

Harvey, Andrew, trans. and adapted. "No End." *Light Upon Light: Inspirations from Rumi*. Berkeley: North Atlantic, 1996.

———. *Son of Man: The Mystical Path to Christ*. New York: Tarcher/Putnam, 1998.

Starhawk (Miriam Simos). *The Spiral Dance: A Rebirth of the Ancient Religion of the Great Goddess*. 20th Anniversary Edition. New York: HarperSanFrancisco, 1999.

Works Consulted

Ackerman, Diane. *Deep Play.* New York: Vintage, 2000.

Barks, Coleman, Trans. *The Essential Rumi.* New York: HarperSanFrancisco, 1995.

Barks, Coleman, Trans. and Michael Green. *The Illuminated Rumi.* New York: Broadway, 1997.

Berry, Thomas. *The Dream of the Earth.* San Francisco: Sierra Club, 1988.

Buber, Martin. *Good and Evil.* Trans. Michael Bullock. New York: Charles Scribner, 1953.

Chodron, Pema. *The Places That Scare You: A Guide to Fearlessness in Difficult Times.* Boston: Shambhala, 2001.

———. *Start Where You Are: A Guide to Compassionate Living.* Boston: Shambhala, 1994.

Christ, Carol P. "Rethinking Theology and Nature." *Weaving the Visions: New Patterns in Feminist Spirituality.* Eds. Judith Plaskow and Carol P. Christ. San Francisco: Harper & Row, 1989. 314-325.

Dalai Lama (Tenzin Gyatso). *The Power of Compassion: A Collection of Lectures by His Holiness the XIV Dalai Lama.* Trans. Geshe Thupten Jinpa. San Francisco: Thorsons, 1981.

———. *The World of Tibetan Buddhism: An Overview of Its Philosophy and Practice.* Trans., ed., and annotated by Geshe Thupten Jinpa. Boston: Wisdom 1995.

Dalai Lama and Howard C. Cutler. *The Art of Happiness: A Handbook for Living.* New York: Riverhead Books, 1998.

Dass, Ram and Mirabai Bush. *Compassion in Action: Setting Out on the Path of Service.* New York: Bell Tower, 1992.

Dossey, Larry. *Healing Words: The Power of Prayer and the Practice of Medicine.* New York: HarperSanFrancisco, 1993.

Doyle, Brendan. *Meditations with Julian of Norwich.* Santa Fe: Bear, 1983.

Fox, Matthew. *The Coming of the Cosmic Christ: The Healing of Mother Earth and the Birth of a Global Renaissance.* New York: HarperSanFrancisco, 1988.

———. *Creation Spirituality: Liberating Gifts for the Peoples of the Earth.* New York: HarperSanFrancisco, 1991.

———. *Original Blessing: A Primer in Creation Spirituality.* Santa Fe: Bear, 1983.

———. *Passion for Creation: The Earth-Honoring Spirituality of Meister Eckhart.* Rochester, VT: Inner Traditions, 1980, 2000.

———. *The Reinvention of Work: A New Vision of Livelihood for Our Time.* New York: HarperSanFrancisco, 1994.

———. *Sins of the Spirit, Blessings of the Flesh: Lessons for Transforming Evil in Soul and Society.* New York: Harmony, 1999.

———. *A Spirituality Named Compassion: And the Healing of the Global Village, Humpty Dumpty and Us.* New York: HarperSanFrancisco, 1979.

Gibran, Kahlil. *The Prophet.* New York: Knopf, 1956.

Grof, Christina and Stanislav Grof. *The Stormy Search for the Self: A Guide to Personal Growth through Transformational Crisis.* New York: Tarcher/Putnam, 1990.

Harvey, Andrew. *The Direct Path: Creating a Journey to the Divine Using the* World's Mystical Traditions. New York: Broadway, 2000.

———. *The Return of the Mother.* Berkeley: Frog, 1995.

———. *Son of Man: The Mystical Path to Christ.* New York: Tarcher/Putnam, 1998.

———. *The Way of Passion: A Celebration of Rumi.* Berkeley: Frog, 1994.

Harvey, Andrew, trans. and adapted. *Light Upon Light: Inspirations From Rumi.* Berkeley: North Atlantic, 1996.

Helminski, Kabir. *Living Presence: A Sufi Way to Mindfulness and the Essential Self.* New York: Tarcher, 1992.

Kasl, Charlotte. *A Home for the Heart: Creating Intimacy and Community with Loved Ones, Neighbors, and Friends.* New York: HarperCollins, 1997.

Kaufman, Gershen and Lev Raphael. *Coming Out of Shame: Transforming Gay and Lesbian Lives.* New York: Doubleday, 1996.

Keck, L. Robert. *Sacred Quest: The Evolution and Future of the Human Soul.* West Chester, PA: Chrysalis Books, 2000.

Keen, Sam. "The Enemy Maker." *Meeting the Shadow: The Hidden Power of the Dark Side of Human Nature.* Eds. Connie Zweig and Jeremiah Abrams. Los Angeles: Jeremy Tarcher, 1991. 197-202.

Leonard, Linda. "The Dark Night of the Soul: Depression and the Veil of Addiction." *Sacred Sorrows: Embracing and Transforming Depression.* Eds. John Nelson and Andrea Nelson. New York: Tarcher/Putnam, 1996. 51-55.

Merton, Thomas. *A Search for Solitude: Pursuing the Monk's True Life.* Ed. Lawrence Cunningham. New York: HarperCollins, 1996.

Moore, Thomas. *Care of the Soul: A Guide for Cultivating Depth and Sacredness in Everyday Life.* New York: HarperPerennial, 1992.

———. *The Re-Enchantment of Everyday Life.* New York: HarperCollins, 1996.

———. *The Soul of Sex: Cultivating Life as an Act of Love.* New York: HarperCollins, 1998.

Myss, Caroline. *Anatomy of the Spirit: The Seven Stages of Power and Healing.* New York: Three Rivers, 1996.

Newton, Michael. *Destiny of Souls: New Case Studies of Life Between Lives.* St. Paul: Llewellyn, 2000.

Nhat Hanh, Thich. *Going Home: Jesus and Buddha as Brothers.* New York: Riverhead, 1999.

O'Murchu', Diarmuid. *Reclaiming Spirituality.* New York: Crossroad, 1999.

Peck, M. Scott. *Further Along the Road Less Traveled: The Unending Journey Toward Spiritual Growth.* New York: Simon & Schuster, 1993.

———. *People of the Lie: The Hope for Healing Human Evil.* New York: Touchstone, 1983.

Roberts, Elizabeth and Elias Amidon, Eds. *Earth Prayers from Around the World: 365 Prayers, Poems, and Invocations for Honoring the Earth.* New York: HarperSanFrancisco, 1991.

Sanford, John. "Dr. Jekyll and Mr. Hyde." *Meeting the Shadow: The Hidden Power of the Dark Side of Human Nature.* Eds. Connie Zweig and Jeremiah Abrams. Los Angeles: Jeremy Tarcher, 1991. 29-34.

Schneider, John. *Finding My Way: Healing and Transformation through Loss and Grief.* Colfax, WI: Seasons, 1994.

Small, Jacquelyn. *The Sacred Purpose of Being Human: A Healing Journey Through the 12 Principles of Wholeness.* Deerfield Beach, FL: Health Communications, 2005.

St. John of the Cross. *The Dark Night of the Soul and The Living Flame of Love.* Comp. Robert Van de Weyer. London: Fount, 1995.

Starhawk (Miriam Simos). *The Spiral Dance: A Rebirth of the Ancient Religion of the Great Goddess.* 20th Anniversary Edition. New York: HarperSanFrancisco, 1999.

Steindl-Rast, David. *Gratefulness, the Heart of Prayer: An Approach to Life in Fullness.* Mahwah, NJ: Paulist Press, *1984.*

Storr, Anthony. *The Essential Jung.* Princeton, NJ: Princeton U., 1983.

———. *Solitude: A Return to the Self.* New York: Ballentine, 1988.

Swimme, Brian. *The Universe is a Green Dragon: A Cosmic Creation Story.* Santa Fe: Bear, 1984.

Swimme, Brian and Thomas Berry. *The Universe Story: From the Primordial Flaring Forth to the Ecozoic Era, A Celebration of the Unfolding of the Cosmos.* New York: HarperSanFrancisco, 1992.

Teasdale, Wayne. *The Mystic Heart: Discovering a Universal Spirituality in the World's Religions.* Novato, CA: New World Library, 1999.

Thoreau, Henry David. *Walden, or Life in the Woods.* New York: Signet, 1964.

Uhlein, Gabriele, Ed. *Meditations with Hildegard of Bingen.* Santa Fe: Bear, 1983.

Underhill, Evelyn. *Mysticism: The Nature and Development of Spiritual Consciousness.* Chatham, NY: Oneworld, 1993.

Walsch, Neale Donald. *Conversations with God: An Uncommon Dialogue — Book 1.* Charlottesville, VA: Hampton Roads, 1995.

———. *Conversations with God: An Uncommon Dialogue — Book 2.* Charlottesville, VA: Hampton Roads, 1997.

———. *Conversations with God: An Uncommon Dialogue — Book 3.* Charlottesville, VA: Hampton Roads, 1998.

———. *Friendship with God: An Uncommon Dialogue.* New York: G.P. Putnam's Sons, 1999.

Welwood, John. "Depression as a Loss of Heart: Opening to Healing Through Inner Work." *Sacred Sorrows: Embracing and Transforming Depression.* Eds. John Nelson and Andrea Nelson. New York: Tarcher/Putnam, 1996. 160-167.

Whitmont, Edward. "The Evolution of the Shadow." *Meeting the Shadow: The Hidden Power of the Dark Side of Human Nature.* Eds. Connie Zweig and Jeremiah Abrams. Los Angeles: Jeremy Tarcher, 1991. 12-19.

Zukav, Gary. *The Seat of the Soul.* New York: Fireside, 1989.

BIOGRAPHY

C. Lynn (Carol) Anderson, D.Min., ACSW, completed her doctoral program at the University of Creation Spirituality, where she studied with some of the foremost scholars in the fields of religion and spirituality. Educated and trained in the fields of spirituality, social work, and education, Dr. Anderson offers a fresh voice in capturing the essence of the human/divine experience; she has been described as an "irreverent mystic." C. Lynn currently teaches social work courses at a Michigan university while also working as a clinical social worker on an inpatient psychiatric unit. No stranger to controversy, she is a political activist regarding GLBT issues.

Dr. Anderson grew up surrounded by the corn fields of northern Indiana where she spent much of her childhood exploring the fields, woods, and swamp that encompassed the family home. Vacationing in northern Michigan since infancy, she recognized that this area was her spiritual home with its blessings of lakes, sun, sand, and pine trees, and moved to the area in 1991 where she currently resides with her beloved cat, Murphy.

You may contact the author through her website,
www.sarahscircle.com or at clynnanderson@sarahscircle.com.

Cover photo by C. Lynn Anderson.
Photo taken at the Anderson homestead in North Liberty, Indiana.

Author photo by Toni Poole at www.picturaphoto.com.

Printed in the United States
125824LV00005B/118-135/P